The Greatest Love

"And this is love" (2 John 6)

Book III of the Kalmus Series

Cho Larson

Rimrock, Arizona

Published by Warner House Press of Rimrock, Arizona, USA

Copyright © 2020 Cho Larson
Cover Design and Illustration © 2020 Ian Loudon, OKAY Media
Interior Design © 2020 Warner House Press

All rights reserved. No part of this book may be used or reproduced in any manner whatsoever without written permission, except in the case of brief quotations in critical articles and reviews. For more information, contact

Warner House Press
4410 E Cayuga Lane
Rimrock, AZ 86335
USA

Published 2021
Printed in the United States of America

Cover image used under license from Shutterstock.com.

Song lyrics cited in Chapter 1 meet the guidelines for Fair Use under 17 U.S.C. § 107.

Unless otherwise noted, all scripture quotations are taken from HOLY BIBLE, NEW INTERNATIONAL VERSION®. Copyright © 1973, 1978, 1984 by International Bible Society. Used by permission of Zondervan Publishing House.

Scripture quotations marked ESV are from The Holy Bible, English Standard Version®, Copyright © 2001 by Crossway Bibles, a publishing ministry of Good News Publishers. Used by permission. All rights reserved.

Scripture quotations marked CSB are taken from the Christian Standard Bible®, Copyright © 2017 by Holman Bible Publishers. Used by permission. Christian Standard Bible, and CSB® are federally registered trademarks of Holman Bible Publishers.

Scripture quotations marked NKJV are from the New King James Version®. Copyright © 1982 by Thomas Nelson. Used by permission. All rights reserved.

Scripture quotations marked NLT are from the Holy Bible, New Living Translation, Copyright © 1996, 2004, 2007, 2013, 2015 by Tyndale House Foundation. Used by permission of Tyndale House Publishers Inc., Carol Stream, Illinois 60188. All rights reserved.

26 25 24 23 22 21 1 2 3 4 5

ISBN: 978-1-951890-13-1

Dedicated to 25 years with
My inspiration,
My love,
Susie

*"No eye has seen, no ear has heard,
and no mind has imagined
what God has prepared
for those who love him."*

(1 Corinthians 2:9 NLT)

Table of Contents

Acknowledgments..**iii**

Foreword...**v**

Prelude to The Greatest Love.................................**vii**

Chapter 1: A Love Song Stolen...................................1

Chapter 2: Singing in the Wrong Color.........................9

Chapter 3: The Wind of Love....................................15

Chapter 4: Boundless, Immeasurable Love..................25

Chapter 5: The Depth and Width of God's Love............31

Chapter 6: Love the Lord With all Your Heart..............37

Chapter 7: Love the Lord with All Your Soul...............43

Chapter 8: Love the Lord with all Your Mind..............51

Chapter 9: Love Your Neighbor as Yourself.................59

Chapter 10: Love Your Enemies................................69

Chapter 11: Love's Promise......................................77

Chapter 12: Enduring Love......................................87

Chapter 13: Loving Discipline..................................97

Chapter 14: Perfect Love Promotes Justice.................107

Chapter 15: The Fragrance of Love...........................117

Chapter 16: Love-Inspired Obedience........................123

Chapter 17: Perfect Love Casts out all Fear................129

Chapter 18: Love is a Banner..................................135

Chapter 19: Love That Separates to Make Us Inseparable..................141

Chapter 20: A Love that Gathers..............................147

Chapter 21: A Love Psalm..**155**

Chapter 22: Love the Giver More Than the Gift.....................**163**

Chapter 23: The Greatest Love Song....................................**171**

Chapter 24: Love is Knocking at Your Heart's Door.................**183**

The Greatest of These..**193**

Study Supplement: Learner-Guided Study...........................**197**

Appendix: Definitions..**199**

Acknowledgments

Most of this study guide was researched and written during lockdown, away from my home library study. We planned a two-week trip to help our son with a medical emergency and ended up spending almost four months in Southern California under pandemic restrictions. My thanks to Dana Point for the beautiful harbor, parks, beaches, community gardens, and outdoor spaces that helped ease our exile.

Our grandchildren, Ben and Penny, deserve a thank you for lightening up our days with their antics and unique personalities. Their dad's appreciation for the ironies of life added some much-needed spice. Many thanks to Michael and Tara who opened their doors, refrigerator, and spare room, accommodating us way beyond ordinary hospitality. We also thank those who watched over the homestead during our extended time away.

Thank you to our friends who prayed us through and sent humorous text messages to distract us from all the pandemic disruptions. Thank you to Mark Philpot, for reading sections of the manuscript and offering a historic Hebraic viewpoint on the Scriptures. I'm very grateful for my editor who helped to fix and polish this manuscript. Most of all, thank you to my wife, Susie, for providing inspiration, love, patience, and prayers to get me through to completion of another book.

May the grace of Christ our Redeemer, the loving kindness of our Father in heaven who sent His Son to save us, and the sweet fellowship and communion of the Holy Spirit bless you with an outpouring of His abundant, immeasurable love. Amen.

Foreword

When this book project began, I knew about the love, mercies, and saving grace of our Lord Jesus Christ. And, because of His plentiful forgiveness of my sins, I had a sense of being loved and loving my heavenly Father with great zeal. Then, as I researched, studied, searched the Scriptures and meditated on them, it's as if my understanding of God's love grew from a small trickle like a mountain brook into a surging river of delight.

The goal for this topical study is to provide a fresh look at the most foundational instruction in the Scriptures regarding God's love. This refreshing viewpoint will lend beautiful hues and a plentiful color palette of descriptions and applications on the Lord's greatest commandment. *The Greatest Love* project has taught me how immeasurable the Father's love is for His sons and daughters—greater than human words can describe.

Every segment of these lessons is written to be consistent with the historic, orthodox tenets of Christian faith. There are no new truths here, but there is a great need for God's people to return to our first love and the truths we too often forget.[1] The study chapters are not written with any one denominational audience in mind, but to teach the truths of God's abundant love with enlightenment from the Spirit of Jesus. While this is presented in lesson form and requires basic intellect to understand, the learner will come to see that love in the kingdom of heaven is so much more than an intellectual pursuit.

We'll also learn this is not a יָדַע yâda (sexual) kind of love,[2] but a חֶסֶד cheçed (compassionate) type of love.[3] No limited human intellect can grasp the vastness of God's loving kindness, but we press on to understand the precepts of the holy Scriptures.[4] Learning this is a challenge because His love is neither earned nor deserved, and yet all of humankind benefits from it.

Many Christians pray as Jesus taught us to pray,[5] and from this we know that God forgives us as we forgive others. But His love is offered without conditions, without limits, and then it inspires us to love as we are loved. When we receive heaven's love as our own, it influences us to love others in the same way. The topic of this Bible study is an immeasurable, abundant love beyond what any human language can fully describe or teach. After jumping into this study with both feet, expect to become saturated with heaven's affections.

---

1. Revelation 2:4.
2. Genesis 4:1.
3. Exodus 34:6.
4. Psalm 119:104.
5. Matthew 6:9–15.

Start this study with a prayer: "Lord, open my understanding so that I may know your abundant love." Now, press on to learn and grow in grace and knowledge and to see what great work Almighty God will do in your heart of hearts.

Like any Biblical topic with such a goal, this study begins by showing the need for a contrite heart and our need for the work of the cross of Jesus Christ. Indeed, it is God's kindness that leads and accompanies us to repentance.[6] We live in a world where hate, prejudice, injustice, cruelty, violence, power struggles, and tribalism seem to rule the day. We all want our lives to matter, but the power-hungry and the machines of commerce and government too often steamroll over us.

It's trite to answer the above negatives with: "All you need is love." That's a bumper-sticker kind of solution. It's a pat answer, and a cliché that's paper thin. It's like one click on a heart emoji that's supposed to fix everything. But it never does. Dig into this study with me and let's rise above trite, bumper-sticker kinds of love and enter into the immeasurable love of Christ.

---

6. Romans 2:4.

Prelude to The Greatest Love

Many life, relational, and spiritual lessons were necessary to prepare me for this study. These rough, sandpaper moments taught me that love compels us to give up a part of ourselves, if not all of ourselves. The challenge we often face is to love someone when their offense has cost us dearly. Even if someone doesn't share the family name, God's love inspires us to sacrifice for the good of others, no matter if it was their offence that created the predicament.

Does this kind of sacrifice sound familiar? The greatest love is to lay down one's life for another. But what if the "other" doesn't deserve it? What if the "other" caused us to suffer? Why should I put up with this torment? The whole mess is his fault!

Our Lord Jesus shows the way.

He died for all sin, for all time—the sin of the whole world. He died for undeserving, violent, despicable, horrible people—the sin of all undeserving souls. For such as these, Jesus gave his body to be broken, His blood to be shed on a cruel Roman cross, so that we may be redeemed when, by faith, we believe and receive this great salvation. Those who follow Christ are called to have the same attitude as our Lord Jesus.

When we hear how Jesus suffered over two thousand years ago, the reality of it may seem very remote. But when we offer to suffer and sacrifice because of another person's wrong, and forgive even when they don't deserve it, we walk in Jesus' footsteps in the way of the cross.

For some, it's become a Christian cliché to say that the greatest love is to lay down our life for another. I've heard men brag, "Oh, yeah. I'd put my life on the line for my wife and kids." But, until a man is tested, it may only be a boast. We can't wait for feelings of love to wash over us before we offer our life to serve our spouse, family, or neighbor. There are times when we must buck up, armor up, and march out in love to serve.

The inspiration for this study book may have begun as a sticky note on the first page of Song of Songs in my Bible. The words were stirred by meditations and study on King Solomon's prose. My scribbled note concludes that God desires sweet, loving, and tender intimacy with us, and we must not give ourselves to another because this would be a betrayal of our whole person and an affront to God who loved us first.

When we teach about a loss of spiritual intimacy, we must be reminded that our Father is a God of mercy, grace, forgiveness, cleansing, and restoration. Our Lord Jesus purchased us with His blood sacrifice. He died in our place and for our sin. Our heavenly Father is more than able to take a person who has been violated, even the violent, and change their hearts, minds, and their very nature by the power of the Word and the Holy Spirit. This requires a miracle, and we can be confident in God Almighty who is God of the impossible.

> *Jesus looked at them and said,*
> *"With man this is impossible, but with God all things are possible."*
> (Matthew 19:26)

This study illuminates the beauty, glory, and wonder of God's abundant and immeasurable love poured out for all who receive of His grace and mercy. We'll learn that this love comes at a price, a price that our Lord Jesus paid in full. What we sacrifice for others is miniscule by comparison. We'll come to see that this is love by choice, because Creator God chose to love us in the beginning, at the creation of the world.

The essence of this study is that God's love, lavished upon us, compels us to love in like manner. His love, mercy, and forgiveness make our love-inspired deeds grow to a greater measure and produce a better effect. The Lord Almighty's love is more contagious and viral than anything on earth. Jesus Christ, our Lord, pours out His love into our vessels[7] until it overflows and floods out to all who are around us.

We will learn that the love of God cannot be measured. It's not as if we have benchmarks to show that we have loved. That would be like that guy who tells his wife, "Look, I got you a birthday card, I got us a bottle of wine for our anniversary, I had dinner with your family on Thanksgiving, and I got you a Christmas present; so that proves I love you." Entering into heaven's love is not an achievement with mile markers and a finish line. The law of love planted in our hearts is not legalistic. There's no ten-step plan to get it. It's simply not achievable on our own.

Throughout this study are references to Yashua HaMachiach and Yehovah (Jehovah). These references offer a sense of the historic roots of our faith. In fact, all that is written here has its foundation in the very first words of creation. The love God pours out on us and the flood of His love that saturates us form the essence of this study.

We begin by considering the notes and tunes that swept us along to where we are today. Then, the second study explores how the wrong kind of love affects those who get caught in cultural trends. This is a difficult place to start,

---
7. 2 Timothy 2:21.

but an essential prelude to heaven's love song. It's like bathing a baby before you put on the clean diaper, a fresh little onesie, and a frilly band in her hair.

This study isn't intended to explore every Scripture about love, but to provide a foundation for further study on your own—with your Bible and the Holy Spirit. The study in the study supplement offers an opportunity to launch your own learning experience with the Holy Spirit's help.

If you are not confident in your faith or not sure of your eternal destiny, start with Chapter 24. This study will help you find the Way to a confident assurance of saving faith.

Each study is necessarily written in a vocabulary of faith. If you're not familiar with the spiritual words used to express this faith, please look up the definitions in Appendix #1.

Chapter 1
A Love Song Stolen

Key Scripture:

- "With persuasive words she led him astray; she seduced him with her smooth talk." (Proverbs 7:21)

This first study deals with the way our Creator's gift of love has been corrupted to please our likes and dislikes. It's a hard place to start because, for most of us, it hits close to home. The realities of a defiled love song affect every one of us. Too many Americans have blazed their own path to love. This lesson is a hard pill to swallow. It's a challenging study session, and yet it offers a greater hope. In the end, those who turn from a love of their own making can be made pure and unblemished before the Lord. Forgiven and cleansed, we are free to love and be loved according to truth and light.

The music every generation has enjoyed, and still enjoys, will show us how love has been reshaped over the past several decades. We still like to dance and sing along with the tunes we grew up with, and yet we must consider how they have shaped our lives and attitudes.

A typical kid in "Leave it to Beaver" America had a transistor radio in his jeans pocket and earphone in one ear. A lot of teachers were clueless about the kid in the back row who listened to the radio instead of learning how to conjugate verbs. Rock and Roll was the rage and, with a pocket radio, kids could tune in anywhere.

Their ear phones crooned out a lot of conflicting messages about love. They learned that love is easy, and can change with the wind. The love ballads of the day captured this confusion:

> "Kiss me each morning for a million years.
> Hold me each evening at your side.
> Tell me you'll love me for a million years.
> Then if it don't work out,
> Then you can tell me goodbye."[1]

Chubby Checker taught kids the twist and they danced through the night. They twisted to Fabian's song "Kissin' and Twistin." They did the slow twist, and the "Mess Around" twist. Kids twisted and sang along with

---

1. "Then You Can Tell Me Goodbye," MP3 audio, track 6 on Johnny Rivers, *Last Train to Memphis*, Soul City Records, 1998.

"Shake it up Baby." Then they flocked to Woodstock to experience legal and illegal pleasures, rock music, and free love. Hugh Hefner gratified a generation of men with published images of seductive, airbrushed models in centerfolds that dragged them down with visions of stolen passions.

The 60s were the golden age of Hollywood, when Oscar reached his pinnacle. Paul Newman and Robert Redford ruled the screen. While Mary Poppins delighted with childlike fantasies, mature audiences looked on as James Bond's charms seduced the Bond Girl who, for her betrayal, ended up completely painted with gold. The influence of the TV screen grew and it broke down barriers established in previous generations. Our hearts and minds were swayed as actors and actresses served to model a new lifestyle right before our eyes.

Kids who grew up in the 70s built on these deceptions with a new, improved version. They rocked while the local garage band boomed out, "Hunka, hunka burnin' love." It wasn't enough to promise a forever kind of love and cut loose in the morning after our eyes blinked open. This generation was determined to have their cake and eat it too. All too often, love turned into little more than spontaneous moments of passion.

They felt the boom of the subwoofers in their chests as they searched for love in night scenes at the club. With slow dance music and senses primed with a Manhattan or Tequila Sunrise, desires turned into trysts, and then into lingering pleasures. It was okay if you stole away the affections that belonged to another. A broken heart? That's their problem. Broken homes? Move on, get over it.

This generation ushered in the golden age of pornography, and they wore "Porn Star" t-shirts to feed the trend. They were primed for this. Their attitudes were shaped for this lifestyle because they were schooled with musical missives like:

> "If loving you is wrong
> I don't wanna be right
> If it means sleeping without you
> I don't wanna be right"[2]

The musical beat of the 80's filled impressionable youthful ears with words like:

> "Let's talk about love
> I wanna know what love is, the love that you feel inside
> I want you to show me, and I'm feeling so much love"[3]

---

2. "(If Loving You is Wrong) I don't Want To Be Right," MP3 audio, track 1 on Barbara Mandrell, *Moods*, MCA Nashville Records, 1978.
3. "I Want to Know What Love Is," MP3 audio, track 3 on Foreigner, *Agent Provocateur*, Atlantic Records, 1984.

These were the sing-along tunes guys and gals played on their car's cassette player as they commuted to work. Women who entered the workforce often found themselves pressured by male bosses who sang the wrong tunes. Their supervisors were all too eager to exploit and "show them the ropes." Some were forced to comply, but many stood up and became their own persons. They shattered glass ceilings. Women pushed themselves to balance work, family, and still have time for that night out with the girls. They went for the whole enchilada, but the ingredients included erroneous missives from their songs.

The 80s TV shows offered "Cheers" with sexual undertones added to humorous antics at their favorite local hangout. Magnum P.I. always got his girl, and M.A.S.H. doctors hit on nurses to be their playmates in the supply room.

What about the "wassup" kids from the 90s who were drummed with musical lyrics like:

> "I'm going out tonight, I'm feelin' alright
> Get a little outta line"[4]

Mariah Carey sang out to feed the trend: "I don't know if it's real / But I like the way I feel." No inhibitions. No conditions. It was like, "Yeah I know, my grandmother thinks it's wrong, but she's from the dark ages, right? What does she know about life in the real world? If it feels this good, it's perfect for me. This is my world, my reality, so it's gotta be right."

This generation's president redefined sexual relations to justify his own uninhibited behavior in the White House, and it caught on. The cheating, soiled atmosphere he created redefined intimate games in the night and stained an entire generation. They threw open the gate to the playground and kids were dragged further away from the possibility of true and lasting love.

Dukes of Hazzard dominated the TV signals in the 80s with the Duke brothers' antics, fast cars, and Daisy who used her high-cut "daisy dukes" to sweet-talk diners and get info for the boys. The Dallas TV series with all its greed, moral failures, relationship ins and outs, twists and turns, and who-done-its, exposed a generation to soap-opera-style living.

Millennials learned all about love as they sang along with Beyoncé:

> "Let's go, get on it
> Yes! So crazy right now!"[5]

---

4. "Man! I Feel Like a Woman!" MP3 audio, track 1 on Shania Twain, *Come on Over*, Mercury, 1997.
5. "Crazy in Love," MP3 audio, track 1 on Beyoncé, *Dangerously in Love*, Columbia, 2003.

This fist pumping generation grew up with parents who told them, "You can be anything you want to be. You can do anything you want to do." At home and at school they were encouraged to reach for the best of life, but that may not be what they heard. Mom and dad's unwitting words set kids free to be "so crazy" about what they wanted from life. They were given the right to create their own moral and spiritual standards. They became "Generation Me." Ethics became negotiable. Gender became a matter of their inner sense of themselves. Limits, standards, and long-established cultural pressures were thrown out the window.

The human body, ever more sexualized, needed implants to enhance it. But silicone wasn't enough. As this generation became adults, they bought over 150 million copies of the book *Fifty Shades of Grey*. They were eager to know the desires and impulses of sexual bondage enthusiast Christian Grey. Their newfound freedoms drove them to pursue illicit pleasures. Stars of Hollywood appeared everywhere in the media with a show of skin to stoke fires of desire. Celebrities appeared on award shows and venues like Super Bowl halftime to stir us in our search for love.

This generation grew up in the age of information and no longer needed their parents to tell them what to do or how to do it. Modern day peer pressures were magnified through social media. Bullies adapted to new technology. The 9-11 attacks right on America's ground zero assaulted everyone with new fears. Panic compelled people to compromise their privacy for the sake of security. Material things became less important. Family treasures were just more stuff to clutter up their lives. Traditional status symbols became less relevant. Life experiences and adventures were the pursuit of this generation. They trashed what past generations valued and pursued what sated their personal needs in chaotic times.

The gals sported feathers in their hair and videotaped themselves doing the Harlem Shake to get their parties started. Tattoo shops popped up around town to serve this generation, because body art became the rage. *Friends* episodes entertained their audience with comedic romances, serious and intermittent relationships, and a love child. *Baywatch* turned into *"Babewatch"* and appealed to their viewers with a show of heroic women coming to the rescue.

Then, we regressed to the present day and time. The #MeToo movement exposed the violence and exploitation people learned and practiced over past generations. Exploitive media moguls were arrested, tried, and sentenced. But, at the same time, human trafficking became rampant worldwide. Innocent boys and girls were enslaved to serve the underground sex trade. It became obvious that the cancer of sexual violence was generations-deep, like invasive sinews pressing deep into the bedrock of our culture. People rose up and drew a line: no more exploitive violence. Instead, those bent on vile passions found satisfaction in the darkness of back rooms. As attitudes changed in public, we tried to put all this behind us to make a new world. A revolutionary empire of love became the latest desire. Would there finally be some hope? Is there light on the horizon? This generation would sing a new song and embrace the universe.

"And the stars make love to the universe"[6]

A sensual "ooh" falls from the lips as starlets look to the universe to light a wildfire in the night. We acclaimed ourselves as stars to exalt the universe. We couldn't find real love in the words of the 60s love ballads. That hunk of burning love left us for someone else. The violent exploiters of the 70s ravaged everything they touched and left broken hearts and lives in their wake. The love feelings of the 80s vanished like a puff of smoke in the wind. The uninhibited love of the 90s didn't work out as planned. Men's shirts and short skirt fashions blew away in the wind of time. The crazy love of the Millennials didn't meet the need, because fifty shades are never enough.

This generation confronted selfishness, callousness, and greed. But, because people seldom change, we simply redefined them as good attributes. These self-serving traits would now be thought of as compassionate, empathetic, and generous in this postmodern world. But deep in our souls there lingered a sense of right and wrong.

We no longer pay indulgences to feudal priests to assuage our sin. Instead, we post nice selfies on social media to show how good we are, as if to pay penance. After fifty "likes," our guilt is absolved of all wrongs committed. Our offenses are covered and we're okay because fifty of our friends "like" us.

What used to be a good thing to say became politically incorrect. Bad words became good words. Insults became compliments. Social media didn't help to change human nature at all, but too often amplified the negatives. Over three thousand years ago, Isaiah wrote about this modern dilemma:

"They say that what is right is wrong and what is wrong is right; that black is white and white is black; bitter is sweet and sweet is bitter."
(Isaiah 5:20 TLB)

Reality TV brought the Bachelor and Bachelorette to our home screens to offer viewers a chance for vicarious affections as they watched sexy singles

---
6. "Empire," MP3 audio, track 2 on Shakira, *Shakira*, RCA, 2014.

sample love until they got it right. At-home spectators watched the summer Olympics in Rio de Janeiro. The athletes showed the glory of human strength and speed. The medal winners inspired us to run to the athletic outfitter to buy sportswear so we could look just like the medal winners.

Music, street slang, popular culture, and mass media all play a big part in shaping our lives, dispositions, language, and sexual attitudes. The effect of all these messages over the years is that it became a good thing to fulfill our own desires. Our default mode is "Me First." Our love is self-absorbed and the universe our illusory lover. We lifted ourselves up to be gods and goddesses of love, and the mirror reflected the love in our eyes. Our own feelings and desires ruled our lives, and this chic sexuality permeated every part of our consciousness.

In the next study, we'll turn off our tunes for a few minutes and think about how this has worked out for us. We'll come to realize that, all this time, we've been singing the wrong songs, to the wrong lover, in all the wrong places. We sang along and now the words get stuck in our heads and our heart strings get pulled away from heaven's kind of love. We've got that morning-after feeling of regret as we walk out the door with the weight of waywardness on our shoulders.

These consequences are too much too much to bear. The weight of our sin hangs on us like chains. But there is forgiveness, mercy, and cleansing for those who come to Christ, who paid the penalty for our waywardness.

1. A Love Song Stolen
Q & A

1. Note how this study affected your view of love.

2. Do you ever get songs stuck in your head? How do the lyrics influence your life?

3. What is the difference between committed relational love and passionate love?

My Journal Notes

Chapter 2
Singing in the Wrong Color

Key Scriptures:

- "How shall we sing the LORD's song in a strange land?" (Psalm 137:4 KJV)
- "As heat is reduced by the shadow of a cloud, so the song of the ruthless is stilled." (Isaiah 25:5)
- "By day the LORD directs his love, at night his song is with me—a prayer to the God of my life." (Psalm 42:8)

This study takes an in-depth look at the consequences of our wrong songs. Why would anyone croon in shades of grey when we could sing with heaven's angels in infinite harmonious and colorful notes? Here we will consider how the tunes that tickled our ears imprinted seditious words on our hearts and minds.

The free loving days of the 60s live on in Boomer lifestyles. Sun City, Arizona has one of the highest rates of STDs in the country. Years later, this generation still hasn't learned that casual passions come with a cost. People may never realize that it's not a good idea to leave your heart in San Francisco. Too many people still buy into the lie that what happens in Vegas stays in Vegas. We may try to convince ourselves that these mantras are true, but reality soon comes home to roost. Illicit entanglements linger at great emotional and physical cost. A stolen love is never free.

A tryst is a forgivable sin, but the natural consequences are devastating. The credit card statement comes in the mail all too soon. A doctor visit is followed by diagnosis and needles. Nightmarish dreams continue to haunt us at night in our own bed. Then, attempts to repair broken relationships are as difficult as breaking through cold, steel barriers. Mending a betrayal of trust is as impossible as breaching the iron gates of a fortress.

A brother wronged is more unyielding than a fortified city;
disputes are like the barred gates of a citadel.
(Proverbs 18:19)

We heard the music and sang along with the eight-track player in our car stereo. We heard the lie and believed the lie because we were lying to ourselves. We convinced ourselves to indulge our desires and pleasures in the moment. But, in the morning light, things didn't look so good. It didn't work out, so "goodbye." We bought into a lie, enjoyed a moment of pleasure, burned the bridges behind us, and paid a steep emotional price for our deceits.

In the 70s, right and wrong turned into a matter people decided for themselves. This generation inspired *Self* magazine in their search for an exceptional spirit and energy to lift them up. Physical fitness fueled the fire that burned in them.

In an attempt to limit the cost of these newfound freedoms, this generation's SCOTUS ruled to give women the liberty to make life and death choices for their unborn children. Now they could control the consequences of spontaneous physical encounters. Women could legally choose to control their own future with or without the responsibilities and expense of a child to hold them back and weigh them down. Indeed, they sacrificed God's children on the altar of self-determination. The Old Testament prophet, Ezekiel spoke against these same evils in his day:

> *Confront them with their detestable practices, for they have committed adultery and blood is on their hands. They committed adultery with their idols; they even sacrificed their children, whom they bore to me.*
> (Ezekiel 23:36–37)

A whole generation sang along as if singing the second verse of the same song. They demanded: "show me what love is!" Were they serious? The blind led the blind into a trap of empty feelings and desire. This kind of love is like the flame of a candle, blown out with one little puff of wind. Right before their eyes the smoke wisps away, and it's gone forever—but they were polluted with the soot of the smoke.

They must have thought: "Ya gotta feed this feeling inside," but when nurtured, the impulses demanded even more. This kind of desire, once encouraged, is insatiable and addictive. Our desires turned into ropes and shackles—a proverbial ball and chain. Entire generations were enticed and entrapped and they would drag the chains with them the rest of their lives. This generation's "Me First" created the need for #MeToo.

The offspring of the Boomer generation grew up with the freedom to be whatever they wanted to be and they changed the signs on the public restrooms from "Men" and "Women" to "All Gender." No one provided them with a strong moral foundation. The freedom to make their own choices about religion, ethics, love, and lifestyle became their right. They tried out all fifty shades of gray and found it left them with a void that demanded to be filled. Hollywood continued to further sexualize the body. The popular mantra became: "Show some skin," as body art made its entrance in popular culture. In this generation, true love became more sexualized and moved further away from reality.

At first the shock and fear created by 9-11 turned the hearts of the people to spiritual matters. Church attendance jumped up for a few months, but the religious messages left people with an empty feeling. Our fears soon devolved into curiosity about Middle-Eastern religions, or no religion at all. More often, the religion question on questionnaires got checked with "none."

Violence and exploitation came to a head in the Echo Boomer generation. #MeToo demanded that it stop, but offered no better alternative than "cease and desist." The roots of violence and exploitation were deep in American culture, but no one offered a lasting remedy. American-style love was cheapened to the point that it has no value. We love our dog, our cat, and our kid's hamster. We love our favorite TV show. We love our special restaurant for a dine out date night. We love our house, garden, car, job, or…whatever. We love everything everywhere. We talk about making love as if it's a superficial fancy. Single guys and gals think they've found love when they make love. A sleepover with our special person means we love them, but there is no lasting commitment to support and strengthen love in relationship.

Even Bible translators gave in to the changed meaning of love. They translated the Hebrew word in Genesis 4:1 עַי yâda, "to know," as "to make love." The beauty and depth of this Hebrew word goes way beyond acts of procreation.

Is there a better way, or are we stuck in this downward spiral? This is the path we have chosen for ourselves, but there has to be a better way. The stolen love we found is elusive like smoke and mirrors. The love we desire promised a freedom that, in fact, enslaved its followers in an invasive darkness. Is it possible that what looked so bright, beautiful, and desirable entrapped us in its grip? Did the eye-pleasing fruit, when eaten, poison our whole being? To answer these questions, let's turn the corner and look to God's love—the eternal gift of love.

Heaven's kind of love is a valuable treasure—as costly as a pearl of great price, and we must let go of everything else to have it. We must give up ourselves so that we may gain this true bond of affection. But we don't have to give up our unique and special personalities. Our God-given talents and gifts remain intact. Heaven's treasures make all that we are an even greater benefit to others.

With each step through time, generations have regressed into a greater self-centered focus and the result is spiritual depravity. We turned God's fragrant garden of delights into a polluted playground with its fences torn down. Self-worship, free love, uninhibited affections, passion without cost, and self-satisfying sex are the idols we worship today. We must turn away from these idolatries so that we may enter into God's eternal love.

This is a call to grieve over our rampant idolatry. We must repent of this insincere love.[1] An evil stain covers all of us, and we are called to turn away from it and repent. We have been influenced by musical lyrics and constant media images that proclaim new freedoms. But the suggestive "freedoms" only disguised the chains that would bind us. Popular culture claimed it would free us, but in fact fettered us and brought a ruinous kind of love. It all felt so right, so we figured it must be right—but it was a trap.

Now that we have shed light on the lies and deceptions, Christ's love compels us to turn from these erroneous attitudes. We ate the forbidden fruit of self-worship that incited us to make ourselves into little gods, like stars that worship the universe. The look of love shined in our eyes, but turned to smoke.[2] And in all this we rejected a true, lasting, and redemptive love that would save us from sin's devastation. God's word brings light to our hearts to convince us of our sin and convict us of our sin. The power of the word leads our hearts to repent of depravity, to see our need of Christ, the cross of Jesus Christ, and the power of the resurrected Christ.

We must be like those who caught Peter's message on the day of Pentecost. When they heard the message of the cross and realized their sinful condition, they responded, "What shall we do?"[3] Peter offered the perfect answer: "Save yourselves from this corrupt generation."[4]

When we come to the Throne of Grace with broken hearts and call on the name of the Lord—not only for our own sin and depravity, but for all the sin around us that affects us and those we love—God is always faithful to forgive and cleanse us of our sins, and remove even the stain of them. With contrite hearts we enter into forgiveness, mercy, and we are restored to sweet fellowship with our heavenly Father. We are set free to love as Jesus loved. Now forgiven, shades of grey turn into a bountiful garden abounding with colorful notes. In repentance we are called to die to ourselves and be raised up in the power of the resurrected Christ, so that we may enter into His eternal, immeasurable love—the joy of His salvation.

When our hearts are broken because of our sin, and we repent of our sin, the boundless love of Christ sweeps over us. His loving kindness sets us free to live in keeping with repentance. We are made new creations in Christ.

---

1. Romans 12:9.
2. Matthew 5:27–29.
3. Acts 2:37.
4. Acts 2:40.

If we confess our sins, he is faithful and just and will forgive us our sins and purify us from all unrighteousness.
(1 John 1:9)

2. Singing in the Wrong Color
Q & A

1. What hope do we have after we've totally messed up in love and life?

2. Explain the challenges we face when trying to restore a broken relationship.

3. Why are people so quick to believe a lie?

4. Who or what is the foundation of all truth?

My Journal Notes:

Chapter 3
The Wind of Love

Key Scriptures:

- "I pray that out of his glorious riches he may strengthen you with power through his Spirit in your inner being, so that Christ may dwell in your hearts through faith. And I pray that you, being rooted and established in love, may have power, together with all the Lord's holy people, to grasp how wide and long and high and deep is the love of Christ, and to know this love that surpasses knowledge—that you may be filled to the measure of all the fullness of God." (Ephesians 3:16–19)

- "They are like a man building a house, who dug down deep and laid the foundation on rock. When a flood came, the torrent struck that house but could not shake it, because it was well built." (Luke 6:48)

The foundation of all truth is established in Christ who is the way, the truth, and the life. The focus of this study is the wind of the Spirit as revealed in creation. We'll come to see an immeasurable love that pours out with ever-increasing streams of righteousness and justice. Through the power of the holy Scriptures, we will come face to face with God's holiness, and our eyes will open to the fullness of His abundant love.

This study shows how the wind of the Spirit that was breathed into Adam reveals God's loving attributes. God's boundless love flows out like winds of the Earth to make His righteousness and justice known through all creation. This is the beauty and majesty of God's word that will become evident to the learner in this study. We will come to see the very essence of God's throne and the steadfastness of His rule in the kingdom of heaven—all of which is encompassed in the Father's love.

> *Righteousness and justice are the foundation of your throne;*
> *love and faithfulness go before you.*
> (Psalm 89:14)

The wind of the Spirit breathed into Adam, who was formed from the dust, to lift him up into God's tender care, place him under God's authority, and fill him a sense of justice, uprightness, and truth. This is the essence and likeness of the Father. The Creator established this in the beginning for the good of humankind for all time. These blessings were given to surround the first two created beings and also their progeny, who would fill and subdue the earth. The Holy Spirit breathed this breath of love as a life-giving gift for created beings who would be called by His name.

> *Bring my sons from afar and my daughters from the ends of the earth—*
> *everyone who is called by my name, whom I created for my glory,*
> *whom I formed and made.*
> (Isaiah 43:6–7 ESV)

The Creator imparted His likeness to Adam in the breath of the Spirit. The special characteristics of God's caring nature were implanted in Adam to give him the heart of a caretaker to tend God's creation. These roots were a good beginning, because all of creation is now set upon this same foundation of love for all time.[1] When Adam sinned against God's command to not eat of the fruit of the tree in the middle of the garden, he and all humankind became subject to the power of death, and the creation to decay. All of Adam and Eve's progeny would be born with a vacant space in their soul, like an empty vessel waiting to be filled with the Spirit. Every child would begin life like a listless sail in need of a steady breeze. By the power of the true Gospel, saving faith in Christ Jesus, and by means of the power of resurrection, every empty vessel, every limp sail, could once again be filled with the breath of the Spirit and free from the chains of sin.

> *For the creation waits in eager expectation for the children of God to be revealed. For the creation was subjected to frustration, not by its own choice, but by the will of the one who subjected it, in hope that the creation itself will be liberated from its bondage to decay and brought into the freedom and glory of the children of God.*
> (Romans 8:19–21)

On the sixth day of creation, God breathed into Adam to give him life in the likeness of the Creator. The flow of the Spirit's breath streamed out with elements of mercy. This abundant love set the foundation for the sacrifice that would redeem fallen humankind for all time. The nail marks of Calvary are made evident in the first words of the Hebrew Scriptures: בְּרֵאשִׁית "In the beginning." These divine words establish the Aleph and Tav,[2] the Alpha and the Omega, the beginning and the end, and the One who stands in the midst of the churches. The Divine Word of creation spoke with love-driven grace and mercy. This pointed the way to the crown of thorns, the cursed tree of crucifixion, the Messiah's victorious reign, and the final victory over sin, Satan, and death. The Aleph and Tav reveal Yeshua HaMashiach as the

---

1. Ephesians 3:17.
2. First and last letters of the Hebrew alphabet.

righteous branch of David[3] who is Head of the seven churches.[4] The Son of Man stood in the midst of the seven golden lampstands and held the seven stars in His right hand. The Living One stood as the First and the Last as He instructed the Apostle John to write love letters to each of the churches. The resurrected Christ held the keys of death and hades so that all blood-bought souls would be made inseparable from the Creator's seventh-day rest.

For I am convinced that neither death nor life, neither angels nor demons, neither the present nor the future, nor any powers, neither height nor depth, nor anything else in all creation, will be able to separate us from the love of God that is in Christ Jesus our Lord.
(Romans 8:38–39)

The wind of the Spirit gave the first man the capacity to love God with all his heart, soul, and strength. The lump of earthen minerals the Creator used to form a body for the man had no capacity for love. This mix of materials was like the clay a potter uses to form a vessel for his own purpose. The new creation made from this elemental mix could only lay lifeless on the ground. But when the Spirit breathed life into him, the man became capable of godly affections. Man was made a living soul with the capacity to love the Lord God of all creation.

Love the Lord your God with all your heart and with all your soul and with all your strength.
(Deuteronomy 6:5)

When the Holy Spirit breathed into Adam, the wind of the Spirit gave him life. This wasn't only atmospheric oxygen to make his body come to life. The Spirit breathed into Adam the Creator's likeness. The Spirit's wind filled Adam's body. This sweet breath revealed God's love for this created man—a protective דֶּסֶח cheçed love.[5] The wind instilled in Adam a yearning for communion. The breath of the Spirit established in the first man and in his life companion, Eve, a desire to seek their Creator. Their love was uncorrupted, and not limited to a יָדַע yâda kind of physical attraction.

I love those who love me, and those who seek me find me.
(Proverbs 8:17)

The account of creation reveals the Almighty's love that is beyond measure. It's boundless and as vast as the universe. The fullness of His love is more than human words can describe. The heights of this love are greater than the four winds of the Earth that blow from the farthest reaches of North, South,

---

3. Jeremiah 23:5.
4. Revelation 1:11.
5. Song of Songs 8:6.

East, and West. There is no ocean that could contain the breadth of it. No galaxy is big enough to encompass the vastness of God's love. The life-giving breath and wind of creation offers a glimpse of the power of the Creator's love.

> *Then the LORD God formed a man from the dust of the ground and breathed into his nostrils the breath of life, and the man became a living being.*
> *(Genesis 2:7)*

The Spirit's breath instilled in the first man a delight in the Creator and all His creation so that humankind would care for the earth as commanded. People born on this earth are taught how to prepare the soil, plant, water, nurture the seed, and then learn various methods to harvest the bounty of the earth. God who Provides teaches farmers, ranchers, viticulturists, naturalists, and gardeners how to sustain the earth so it will continue to flourish and produce. It's as if the breath of the Spirit fills all of humankind's baskets and carts with an abundant harvest. Plants to cultivate and bring food from the earth are provided for all humankind. They are taught how to make wine to gladden the heart. They are trained to create ointments to make their faces shine, and grow the grains for bread to sustain their families.[6]

> *The farmer knows just what to do, for God has given him understanding.*
> *(Isaiah 28:26 NLT)*

The wind of the Spirit made Adam fruitful so that he would multiply and fill the earth with righteous offspring. The Creator's desire is for every corner of the created world to be inhabited by His family—those who would walk in communion with Him. Because of this implanted affection, Adam and his progeny were given the task of nurturing God's creation. His offspring would spread throughout the earth to bear godly children and fulfill the Creator's covenant command to subdue the earth.

> *God blessed them and said to them, "Be fruitful and increase in number; fill the earth and subdue it. Rule over the fish in the sea and the birds in the sky and over every living creature that moves on the ground."*
> *(Genesis 1:28)*

The breath of the Spirit placed a distinct aroma in the first man and woman, just as He gave the flowers, trees, and vines special scents for people to enjoy. Adam and Eve, in their unfallen state, surely gave off a sweet fragrance that far exceeded that of the sacrificial animals that would later be offered up for the sin of man.[7] The second Adam, Jesus Christ, would restore this sweet aroma to God's people.

---

6. Psalm 104:14–15.
7. Psalm 66:15.

> *But thanks be to God, who always leads us as captives in Christ's triumphal procession and uses us to spread the aroma of the knowledge of him everywhere. For we are to God the pleasing aroma of Christ among those who are being saved and those who are perishing.*
> (2 Corinthians 2:14–15)

The breath of the Holy Spirit instilled in Adam a heart that desired fellowship. The wind of the Spirit filled Adam's body, soul and spirit so he could walk in sweet communion with God in the garden in the cool of the day. The prophet Ezekiel shows us the power of the wind of the Holy Spirit. The Spirit breathed the four winds into dry bones and they came to life. Tendons, muscle, and skin formed on the dry skeletal remains scattered on the ground. This mighty army of living beings from the prophet's vision were settled in a land where they would know God's voice and recognize the hand of God at work in and through them. They would have the reality of Yahweh's holy presence to permeate their beings and surround them on every side with His loving kindness.

> *"I will put my Spirit in you and you will live, and I will settle you in your own land.*
> *Then you will know that I the LORD have spoken,*
> *and I have done it," declares the LORD.*
> (Ezekiel 37:14)

The Spirit breathed a song into Adam that would overflow from his heart. The gift of music soothed his soul and washed him with sweet peace for his whole being. During Adam's lifetime, the first instruments were made. Jubal is mentioned as the father of all who would play the harp and pipes.[8] Because of the wind of the Spirit placed in Adam, a natural wellspring of thanksgiving flowed out in song. Whether to lament, mourn, celebrate, or express joy and happiness, there will always be a song to express the heart's sentiment because of the Spirit's wind breathed into Adam.

> *As they make music they will sing, "All my fountains are in you."*
> (Psalm 87:7)

The Spirit's wind encompassed Adam like the dew of morning to make him blossom like the flowers of the field, and to send his roots down into the earth where he would walk about for almost a thousand years. The dew of heaven is likened to righteousness that settles to refresh the earth as the dawn's light breaks over the horizon and again as the sun descends in the western sky.

> *May God give you heaven's dew and earth's richness–an abundance of grain and new wine.*
> (Genesis 27:28)

---

8. Genesis 4:21.

Every aspect of the Spirit's wind expressed a longing for, a penchant toward the beings God created in His image. The Creator first loved us so that we may now love Him and delight to walk in the light. This same love is breathed into all those who are made new creations in Christ. This breath of loving kindness is held out to all people today to give them the capacity to love spouse, family, and neighbors. This godly love inspires salt and light for the world,[9] and is the catalyst for creating safe towns and villages where we raise our children. In the safety of community, godly parents can present their children to God Almighty as His own, and this same love compels us to raise them up in the disciplines of Christ-like living.

We love because he first loved us.
(1 John 4:19)

The Spirit of Father God breathed life into Adam. Now, all of humankind is born with a yearning to know their Creator and be filled with the wind of the Spirit. Many have searched for God because of this yearning to pursue knowledge of the Creator and His creation.[10] King Solomon exemplified this pursuit as he "grasped for the wind."[11] The origin of all pursuits of knowledge came about as the Spirit of the Word of creation blew the winds of the North, South, East and West into the nostrils of the first created being. All who search out the mysteries of God; scientific knowledge, education, apprenticeship, history, and instruction in life skills are under the effect of this aspect of the breath of love instilled in Adam, Eve, and renewed again in Christ.

The fear of the LORD is the beginning of wisdom; all who follow his precepts have good understanding. To him belongs eternal praise.
(Psalm 111:10)

The Apostle Paul became an astute student of the Pentateuch.[12] He understood the Spirit's breath of love and he teaches us the effects of the wind breathed into Adam. Paul made it applicable to our everyday lives, and the words he wrote have become the standard for love in Christian wedding ceremonies. Before Adam's fall these attributes were as normal and natural as the rising and setting of the sun. Indeed, love ruled the morning, evening, and through the night hours until stolen away by the deception of the serpent.

---

9. Matthew 5:3–14.
10. Ecclesiastes 3:11.
11. Ecclesiastes 1:14, 17.
12. See the first five books of the Bible.

THE GREATEST LOVE

Love is patient, love is kind. It does not envy, it does not boast, it is not proud.
It does not dishonor others, it is not self-seeking, it is not easily angered, it keeps no
record of wrongs. Love does not delight in evil but rejoices with the truth.
It always protects, always trusts, always hopes, always perseveres.
Love never fails.
(1 Corinthians 13:4–8)

The Creator's wind breathed into Adam the same gift of love Yehovah God offered to His holy nation, Israel. This loving nature given to Adam and Eve would nurture, provide, teach, discipline, and encourage their offspring, just as the Creator did for them. This is the longing Christ has for His Church today—the sheep of his pasture. A lily flower gives us an illustration of this principle: The early morning breezes carry dew to the lily and it absorbs the humidity to help it grow and blossom. And then, when the flower opens, it spreads its sweet fragrance.

I will be like the dew to Israel; he will blossom like a lily.
Like a cedar of Lebanon he will send down his roots;
his young shoots will grow.
His splendor will be like an olive tree, his fragrance like a cedar of Lebanon.
People will dwell again in his shade; they will flourish like the grain,
they will blossom like the vine–
Israel's fame will be like the wine of Lebanon.
(Hosea 14:5–7)

The wind of the Spirit gives us strength to walk in God's pathway, to serve Him, and worship Him with our whole being. All of us in God's creation need the light of the fourth day of creation to illuminate a path for our feet. Even more than this, we need the light of the first day of creation to enlighten our inner being to love Creator God and walk in His ways. This is the delightfully obedient kind of love breathed into the first Adam by the wind of the Spirit.

The Second Adam, Jesus Christ, breathes this same light and love into fallen creatures who repent and are redeemed by the blood of the sacrificial Lamb of God who takes away the sin of the world. The Second Adam, Jesus Christ, forgives and cleanses all redeemed men, women, and children, and once again breathes into them the capacity for love and obedience. In Christ, all new creations are made in the likeness of the Creator.[13] Restored souls have the means to love the Lord God with their whole heart. But, like the first Adam, we are fallible and often fail in obedience. When we trip up, we can be confident that the Father's long-suffering love compels Him to wait for us to return.[14]

---
13. 1 Corinthians 15:49.
14. Luke 15:20.

> *But be very careful to keep the commandment and the law that Moses the servant of the* L`ORD` *gave you: to love the* L`ORD` *your God, to walk in obedience to him, to keep his commands, to hold fast to him and to serve him with all your heart and with all your soul.*
> (Joshua 22:5)

Every structure needs a solid foundation to stand firm. This sure foundation serves its purpose when earth shakes. What we build upon the Rock is eternal and cannot be thrown down. A realm as vast as the kingdom of heaven requires a most sure foundation to be unshakeable. The basis of all good things in the universe became established in the first seven days of creation. When the Holy Spirit breathed life into the first man, Adam, He placed him in agreement with all creation. Once again, by means of the cross of Jesus Christ, all redeemed people may serve and flourish in God's created world.

The wind of the Spirit breathed into Adam a sense of justice, and a desire to search out the mysteries of the Creator. All people upon whom the Spirit breathes new life become the salt of the earth and the light of the world. This salt and light is the basis of efficient commerce on this green orb, the productive farms and factories, and orderly management of towns and villages. Indeed, the Spirit's breath instilled in humankind in the beginning is renewed for us in Jesus Christ by the breath of the Holy Spirit.

The nurturing love men and women have for each other, for family, friends, and neighbors was all made possible by the Spirit's breath in the first man and now restored to redeemed souls in the Spirit of Christ. The desire to care, nourish, and provide for our children entered into the human race as the wind of the Spirit breathed into the lump of clay the Creator formed on the sixth day. Like the morning and evening dew that falls on the earth, all righteousness was established in the beginning, and is now renewed in all new creations in Christ in whom the Spirit's wind is breathed.[15] It is by faith in Jesus Christ as Lord and Savior that the foundation of God's boundless love is restored in those who are called by His holy name.

---

15. 1 Corinthians 2:7.

3. The Wind of Love
Q & A

1. Why is the Creator's love such an integral a part of redemption?

2. How does God's love, breathed into redeemed souls, affect all humankind?

3. Describe love as God created it to be in the beginning.

4. What is the fragrance of love?

My Journal Notes

Chapter 4
Boundless, Immeasurable Love

Key Scriptures:

- "My mouth will proclaim your righteousness, and your salvation all day long. Though I don't grasp its full measure." (Psalm 71:15)[1]
- "And I pray that you, being rooted and established in love, may have power, together with all the Lord's holy people, to grasp how wide and long and high and deep is the love of Christ, and to know this love that surpasses knowledge—that you may be filled to the measure of all the fullness of God." (Ephesians 3:17–19)

How far is East from the West? If you try to make them come together, your head will start to spin. Fly east on this planet and you will never come to a point where you'll start to travel west. If we set our compass to go west, we will continue west until we make a 180-degree turn. The expanse between east and west is limitless—they never intersect. But God's love is greater than this unlimited distance.

The Father's infinite, loving nature is clearly taught in the Scriptures. The Psalmist teaches that God's love is as high as the heavens above the earth. If you look at the universe through the Hubble telescope, how far could you see into space? God's love is a greater measure than the 46.5 billion light years of the observable universe. Some scientists estimate the entire dimensions of the universe to be fourteen trillion light years—but even that number is inadequate to measure an ever-expanding creation and God's abounding love for His created beings.

God's vast, immeasurable creation with all its amazing expanses of multicolored splendor, the constantly revolving galaxies, flaming stars, and planets that orbit with the seasons of time are a wonder to behold. But all this together cannot compare with the Creator's immeasurable love and mercies for those who are called by His name.

For as high as the heavens are above the earth, so great is his love for those who fear him; as far as the east is from the west, so far has he removed our transgressions from us.
(Psalm 103:11–12)

God's love-inspired grace is more extravagant than the human mind can comprehend. Saul, who was also called Paul, offers himself as an example of

---
1. Author's translation based on Hebrew text.

God's bountiful love, grace, mercy, and forgiveness. Saul studied under the renowned Gamaliel and became an ardent student of the Talmud and Torah. He lived a perfectly pious life with regard to the letter of Hebraic Law. But he was not "circumcised of heart."[2] His violent attitude violated the spirit of the Law.

Because of this spiritual blindness, Saul rose up against the Spirit of Christ and His body, the Church. He stood in agreement as the crowd picked up rocks to stone Stephen, a deacon of the church, after his bold proclamation of faith in Jesus the Messiah. And from that moment, it's as if an ungodly rage rose up in him and he began to torment Jesus' followers. Saul arrested and condemned to death many of the first Christians. With a letter in hand from the High Priest in Jerusalem, he marched off to Damascus to arrest more Christians. He planned to murder Jesus' followers because of his hated for the Christian faith. He literally persecuted Christ as he condemned to death people who confessed faith in Him.

Paul later admitted to his past as a blasphemer, persecutor, and a violent man.[3] Because of the threats of Saul's hostility breathed out against them, Christians throughout the region were concerned, but willing to put their lives on the line for Christ. It's not difficult to imagine Saul's face twisted with a dark and violent rage against simple people who had come to saving faith in Jesus.

Saul's exceptional education in Rabbinic religious tradition didn't prevent his ignorance and unbelief. He violently rose up against what he considered a religious sect that threatened the institutions he served. Traditions established by men incited his raging indignation toward the Church.

Could anyone be a better example to display our Lord and Savior's immeasurable love-inspired grace, mercy, and forgiveness? Could there be a more fitting illustration of Christ's power to save? The radiant light of Christ dramatically called Saul out of the darkness of horrible and violent sins.[4] Christ's forgiveness instilled a passion for the Gospel of Jesus Christ in Saul who became known as the Apostle Paul. As a forgiven soul, Paul loved the One who pardoned him more than ever possible.[5] With his zealous rage cleansed, the old Saul became dead to sin. His wicked self died, his zealous violence perished, and Christ Jesus raised him up a new man in the power of resurrection. Now forgiven and cleansed, the Spirit of Jesus empowered this new man. The effect was Paul's zealous love for Christ and His church. Once responsible for so many deaths, this man would now serve to lead people to Christ. The converts in Paul's day added to all converts through the rest of

---

2. Deuteronomy 30:6.
3. 1 Timothy 1:13.
4. Acts 22:6.
5. Luke 7:47.

time will be as "numerous as the stars in the sky and as countless as the sands on the seashore."[6]

What sins have captured you? What form of darkness has its grip on you? Are you foul-mouthed? Addicted? Divorced? Unfaithful? Deceptive? Violent? Adulterous? Hateful? Abusive? A liar? Thief? Murderer? Prostitute? Slave driver? Cheater? Malcontent? If you are all of the above over and over, again and again, but then become broken before Christ and repent of your sin, you can be made a whole new creation in Christ. When you repent and turn away from sin there is an immeasurable, love-driven abundance of grace, mercy, and forgiveness sufficient to redeem a repentant heart from the condemnation of these sins and to bring a contrite soul into the realm of God's mercy. You may think: "I'm not any of the above." But everyone born into this fallen world, through no fault of their own, becomes part of a sin-bent world; a slave to sin in need of freedom in Christ.[7]

Whether we are guilty of few or many sins, the evils that once burdened us are revealed in the light. But what we tried to cover up can be washed away in the blood of Christ.

God's loving justice requires judgment against sin. God's warning to the first man, Adam, established that the punishment for sin against a holy God must be death.[8] But God provided a remedy, and that is Christ and the cross of Jesus Christ. He is the Lamb of God who paid the penalty for sin. If we confess our sin, God who is faithful and just will forgive us of all our sin, cleanse us from the burden of the offences, and even wash away the stains of our depravity.[9] Our new life in Christ will be like the bright whiteness of freshly fallen snow.[10] As a new and different person in Christ, we will be given a white stone of absolution with our new name written on it.[11]

This miracle is possible because of the immeasurable love poured out from the Throne of Grace upon all who will hear the truth of the Gospel, grasp the truths of the kingdom of heaven, and then come into covenant with Jesus who is the way, the truth, and the life. When we hear this true Gospel, the seed of faith is planted in our hearts. Then, in the miraculous power of heaven's baptism, we die to sin and self to be raised up in the power of the resurrected Christ—a whole new creation in Christ. All this is made possible because of the love of our Lord Jesus.

---

6. Hebrews 11:12.
7. 1 John 1:8.
8. Romans 6:23.
9. 1 John 1:9.
10. Isaiah 1:18.
11. Revelation 2:17.

> *The grace of our Lord was poured out on me abundantly,*
> *along with the faith and love that are in Christ Jesus.*
> (1 Timothy 1:14)

The mighty Mississippi River begins as a trickle flowing out of Lake Itasca in Northern Minnesota and grows in breadth and depth, fed by mighty tributaries, until it finally pours 1.6 million gallons per second into the salt waters of the Gulf of Mexico. Even the powerful flow of this river is less than a drop when compared to the river of righteousness that flows from the throne of God who is Most High over all the earth. May God be glorified because of this abundant love.

What would it be like to float along on the ever-increasing current of heaven's river? What started as a flow of blood and water from Jesus' side as he was pierced while hanging on the cross has now become a river too vast and powerful to measure—a flood, a wave of love-driven righteousness. It is the means of righteousness and the ripples of Christ's uprightness that will finally and forever bring God's creation under Jesus' feet.[12] In this love-inspired justice, the whole earth will be covered with dew from God's holy mountain. By the awesome power of righteousness, the whole Earth will be made subject to the King above all kings, and the Lord who is above all lords. With justice and righteousness poured out, the earth will flourish like pomegranates and be filled with the sweetness of heaven. The lilies of the field will blossom in all their glory. Pasturelands will grow rich and fertile. The fig tree will once again bear its good fruit. Waves of golden grain will be gathered and earth's meadows will thrive like the garden of God. All this is possible because of God's all-encompassing love for those who are made in His image.

> *But let justice roll on like a river, righteousness like a never-failing stream!*
> (Amos 5:24)

The full measure of our Salvation is an unknown as vast as the universe. Is it possible that we will explore the infinite mysteries of Father God, His kingdom, and the wonders of the new heaven and earth forever? Indeed, the vastness of the Creator's glory, majesty, and splendor may keep us occupied as we discover new things for an eternity.

Can we number the stars in the heavens above? Even if you could see them all, you couldn't count them. We can barely comprehend numbers in the millions, billions and trillions. But when we get into quadrillions and nonillions, these numbers are way beyond what we can grasp. So, how is it possible to comprehend the overwhelming love shown to us by God of our

---

12. 1 Corinthians 15:25.

Salvation? The Lord's awesome glory is beyond measure—beyond our ability to comprehend. And yet, the treasures of the heavenly realm are far greater than the many good things in God's natural creation.

4. Boundless, Immeasurable Love
Q & A

1. What words will you use to describe the full measure of God's love?

2. Why is the Apostle Paul a good example of God's loving grace and mercy?

3. Describe Saul before and Paul after God called him. What made the difference?

4. Describe the human capacity for love. What is the source of this love?

My Journal Notes:

Chapter 5
The Depth and Width of God's Love

Key Scripture:

- "Can you fathom the mysteries of God? Can you probe the limits of the Almighty? They are higher than the heavens above—what can you do? They are deeper than the depths below—what can you know? Their measure is longer than the earth and wider than the sea." (Job 11:7–9)

In this study, we'll explore examples from God's creation to help us see its grandeur. The reality of this beautiful, vast universe is greater than what our minds can completely comprehend. Consider the musical notes the human ear can hear. We can only pick up about ten octaves, but there is no limit to sounds in the universe or the notes sung out in heaven's songs.[1] Surely many thousands of angels sing a range of notes and harmonies beyond our comprehension.

There may be more than eighteen decillion colors in God's created universe, but the human eye can only perceive about seven million colors, hues, and shades. Human olfactory systems can detect about one trillion odors, aromas, and fragrances, but even our dog has more smell receptors. Try to imagine the abundant fragrances that will waft from the garden of God.

The human capacity for love seems to grow when a new baby comes home to be a part of the family. The gift of a special-needs child born into a household makes our love blossom, flourish, and strengthen like no other. When man and wife are joined together to be wedded before God and witnesses, the Father's love strengthens their affections and causes them to overflow with delight.

There are ten basic human emotions, and possibly a total of thirty, but all are limited by the capacity of mortal beings. The love we come to know through life events can't compare to the infinite love God has shown us. Try to imagine the height, depth, and breadth of emotions without the limitations of earthbound fallen humanity. The contrast of human love to God's infinite love for all His created beings gives us a picture of our inability to comprehend the unlimited, immeasurable love of our Lord and Savior.

The above illustrations leave us with a sense of our limited human understanding. Our minds can't apprehend the boundless love that compelled our Lord Jesus to give His life as a ransom to pay the penalty of our sin. Consider His love for us. He was arrested, falsely accused at an illegal trial, abandoned

---
1. Revelation 5:11–12.

by His disciples, condemned to death by hateful shouts of the crowds, beaten and bruised, and a crown of thorns pressed onto His head. He was flogged with a Roman cat-of-nine-tails, forced to carry His own cross, and then His hands and feet nailed to rough-cut, wooden beams. But even as He gasped to breathe, He spoke words of forgiveness over those who condemned Him to death because they didn't know what they were doing. The passion of Christ is the greatest expression of love ever witnessed. But His love for us continues to grow. The love of Christ lifts us up to greater love as He extends to us His rod of comfort. He draws us into the kingdom of the Son with all its benefits, protections, and glorious wonders.

Greater love has no one than this: to lay down one's life for one's friends.
(John 15:13)

Creator God established all righteousness in the beginning as He created heaven and earth. Indeed, all of creation is founded in God's love. These origins are restored in Christ, the Second Adam, so that we may bear the fruit of the Creator's abundant love. The wonders of His love are greater than the created universe and more than mind, heart, soul, and spirit can fully comprehend.

If a student were to commit herself to a lifetime of research and study of God's love, this would not be enough time to learn, write, and teach the overwhelming abundance of the Lord's affections toward His created beings. Such a researcher would grow in grace and knowledge in her life-long pursuit, and yet there would remain greater heights to reach for every day of her life.

What if a carpenter took out his laser tape measure in an attempt to determine the full dimensions of the Almighty's abundant love? He would find himself in an endless pursuit more impossible than to measure every square inch of the 400,000 square feet of the Antilla mansion in India. We simply can't quantify love. True love isn't gauged by dozens of roses in her favorite color to fill every room of the house with fragrance. Affections aren't determined by mountains of Hallmark cards sent to him with affectionate rhymes. Gifts of gold, silver, and pearls to our loved one, though they fill the house, could not quantify love. Wining and dining our date at the best restaurants in town aren't a good measure of love. Indeed, love can only be measured by what it produces.

What if a young man falls in love and spends a lifetime writing and singing more and more verses of a serenade to his lover? What if he wrote countless pages of musical score to express his devotion? All this would never live up to the full standard of the Creator's love for His own.

All the love and affection expressed in the examples above are possible because our roots are set in God's love as revealed in all of creation. The Creator's love grows deep in us and for all humankind. How great, how wonderful, how abundant is this love shown to us by our Father in heaven, Creator of all the heavens and earth.

I pray that you, being rooted and established in love, may have power, together with all the Lord's holy people, to grasp how wide and long and high and deep is the love of Christ, and to know this love that surpasses knowledge–
that you may be filled to the measure of all the fullness of God.
(Ephesians 3:17–19)

The vast wealth of God's loving kindness is greater than all the words ever written. Indeed, if all of Jesus' acts of love as He served among us were written down, the world could not contain the books that would be written.[2] Jesus patiently touched and healed those who came to Him with their infirmities and troubles. At one point in Immanuel's time among us, He expressed this long-suffering patience. He wondered out loud how long He would have to put up with the crowd's unbelief.[3]

Jesus' liberal expressions of love were evident in His patient and compassionate ministries. He spent over three years preparing the disciples to carry on His work with the same patient love. This legacy of immeasurable affection is given to us so we can continue the Great Commission in the power of His abundant and patient love.

The Lord is not slow in keeping his promise, as some understand slowness. Instead he is patient with you, not wanting anyone to perish,
but everyone to come to repentance.
(2 Peter 3:9)

The magnificent beauty, depth, width, and length of the Grand Canyon that stretches across northern Arizona isn't grand enough to contain the bountiful love God has lavished upon humankind. Consider the awesome waters of the Columbia River that flow from the Rocky Mountains in British Columbia, Canada. This river's powerful current produces hydropower for cities to thrive, provides water for fields and farmlands of the Columbia basin, carries barges laden with grain, and finally flows into the Pacific Ocean with sufficient depth and width for ocean going ships to navigate. All the natural wonders of the world, the great rivers, lakes, and ocean tides, are but a drop when compared to the love God has poured out on His creation.

---

2. John 21:25.
3. Luke 9:41.

When love-inspired righteousness comes to its full measure, it will cover the earth as the dew of God's holy mountain and "the earth will be filled with the knowledge of the glory of the Lord as the waters cover the sea."[4] The fruit of this love-driven righteousness is that God's people are rooted and grounded in love, awash in love, and saturated in God's love.

This boundless, immeasurable love provides forgiveness for the guilt of sin that binds us like ropes. The ball and chain we've dragged with us all our lives is broken loose by the power of forgiveness. Christ's love, mercy, and grace are poured out on us in abundance to wash us clean as fresh fallen snow. Salvation is ours because of God's infinite love poured out upon unworthy souls.

We are not called to salvation because we've been wonderful people, but because our Lord and Savior has called us and chosen us. As the foundation of all creation was set in place, Creator God knew our names. He made note of our names, and chose to pour out His love upon us.

How could we deny so great a love?[5]

5. The Depth and Width of God's Love
Q & A

1. Describe how the dew of righteousness comes to full measure and then fills the earth with God's glory.

2. Does Jesus' loving sacrifice lift you up to a greater love?

3. Describe the wonders of God's loving kindness that are written on your heart.

4. What words are inspired in your soul to begin writing a love song for your Lord and Savior?

---

4. Habakkuk 2:14.
5. See Chapter 24.

My Journal Notes:

Chapter 6
Love the Lord With all Your Heart

Key Scriptures:

- "I pray that out of his glorious riches he may strengthen you with power through his Spirit in your inner being, so that Christ may dwell in your hearts through faith. And I pray that you, being rooted and established in love, may have power, together with all the Lord's holy people, to grasp how wide and long and high and deep is the love of Christ, and to know this love that surpasses knowledge—that you may be filled to the measure of all the fullness of God." (Ephesians 3:16–19)

Most people can see that love and heart go together like hand and glove, peanut butter and jelly, or a hamburger sandwiched in a sesame seed bun. It's as if they come together in harmony. In this study, we'll learn what it means to love the Lord with all our whole heart. This is a love-inspired command, and, as we follow this instruction, we will become awash with many good things that affect everyone around us.

In American culture, the heart has become an emoji that means "like," "cool," or "awesome." We ♡ NY, we ♡ our friend's posts on Facebook, and we ♡ the family pictures on Instagram. In fact, we ♡ almost everything including our beagle puppy and our favorite TV show. ♡ is so overused it has become meaningless. It's like diluting a vintage wine with tap water. The emotions expressed by our ♡ emojis are as shallow as the puddle our beloved puppy left on the floor. Our colored ♡ emojis become as transitory as a child's face painting that's washed off before bedtime.

Physical reality is that the heart is a muscle to pump blood and circulate oxygen and nutrients through the body. The spiritual reality is that the heart of a person is considered the nucleus for our emotions, especially human affections. The practical reality is that desires, delights, passions, anger, and all our emotions get poured out on those around us. Our heart pours out with truth and light or lies and darkness. All this comes from the very essence of our being. What is in our heart affects everyone around us, most of all those closest to us.

But there is hope for emotional creatures. Our heavenly Father understands human needs. He gives us wine to make our hearts glad.[1] He gives us music to express the joy that overflows from our hearts and makes our feet

---
1. Psalm 104:15.

dance. The words spoken from our mouths ought to overflow from a pure heart to spread heaven's blessings in word and song. Best of all, singing out with a cheerful song heals body and soul better than any prescription,[2] and the side effects are always excellent.

The good person out of the good treasure of his heart produces good, and the evil person out of his evil treasure produces evil, for out of the abundance of the heart his mouth speaks.
(Luke 6:45 ESV)

There's also the down side of life that creates another range of deep emotion. When we lose a loved one, we grieve because of that empty place in our heart. When we see our children suffer, our heart goes out to them and we suffer with them. We feel grumpy when we don't get our morning coffee. We get impatient when our stomach growls from the aroma of hamburgers on the grill, and the server ignores us. We get angry when someone offends us. We're terribly frightened when we get separated from our kids in a crowd. All of these emotions come from the heart, and for this reason our Father offers comfort for our hearts. He sends help in the form of guardian angels who lead our kids back to us. Then He provides comfort food—a cinnamon roll with cream cheese frosting to settle us down. And when we feel blue, our hearts may inspire a sorrowful song to sing.

Abba Father comforts our hearts, but His tender consolations don't stop with those who are consoled. His solace overflows like a fountain and splashes on everyone around us. His love overflows from our hearts to compel a search for treasure in the Scriptures and store it up to know true wisdom. This deep, from-the-heart kind of wisdom leads us to live our lives as an extension of true worship. By the power of wisdom, we will take captive and discard the erroneous thoughts that spring up from within. The thousands of messages and images constantly thrown at us in this media-frenzied world get filtered by hearts of wisdom. Heaven's wisdom gives us eyes to see other people for who they are, rather than objects to please us. A heart of wisdom leads us to repentance and to confess our wrongs before a holy God, and then receive His mercy and forgiveness.

We demolish arguments and every pretension that sets itself up against the knowledge of God, and we take captive every thought to make it obedient to Christ.
(2 Corinthians 10:5)

To set our feet on a foundation of wisdom we must go back to the very beginning of creation's story. God established His creation in love. The Old Testament covenant was instituted in love as if from the very heart of the

---
2. Proverbs 17:22.

Word of creation. The basis of the Law is to love the Lord God with all our heart, soul, and mind. The Hebrew word בַּל "lêb" or "Lev" means "heart." This word infers that the book of Leviticus is the Law from the heart of God. Then, under the New Covenant, this law of love is written on the hearts of God's people.[3]

What does it mean to put our whole ♡ into loving God? What color is the ♡ that loves God completely? How many ♡s do we have to click to love God passionately? How dark is a ♡ that feels heavy with grief? With all our ♡ emojis, we have diluted what is real and our affections become shallow and meaningless.

We can go beyond this shallowness and enter into a God-inspired love that will flow out from the essence of our being. It will spring up from the depths of who we are in Christ. This kind of love is colored by our emotions and affections. A heart grounded in love makes it possible for us to love the Lord God in every circumstance, even when we are angry, sad, or grumpy. The words that flow from our hearts and out of our mouths are like sweet fruit from the vine that reveals the love we have for our Lord and Savior. These heartfelt expressions are like pure gold. A heart of refined gold makes our feet walk on paths of righteousness and justice. The deep treasures of a wise heart will flood out with heaven's riches, with honor and prosperity.

My fruit is better than fine gold; what I yield surpasses choice silver.
(Proverbs 8:19)

We are called to love Father God from the depths of our heart. With every sentiment we honor our heavenly Father. All our affections will reflect our love of Abba Father and His love for us. He gives us songs for our hearts that make our feet dance, and then we can welcome a partner to join us so their feet can dance too. Savory biscuits smothered in gravy may comfort our stomachs, but even better to offer solace from our hearts to others in need. Wine is a gift to make our hearts glad, and we share this gladness with friends and neighbors. In all these good things, we receive and give in like manner because of our love for the Lord Almighty.

In reality, for all who are part of this fallen human race, complete, heartfelt love toward our Creator is beyond our capacity. It is only made possible in the realm of the Spirit of Christ and by means of His redemptive power. When we come to saving faith and are born of living water and the word, we are made new creations in Christ, circumcised of heart. We die to ourselves and are raised up in the power of the resurrected Christ so that we may love

---
3. Jeremiah 31:33.

the Lord God with all our hearts.

Actions that flow from a pure heart are the effect of this genuine love. It's as if loving the Lord with all our hearts goes full circle. First, our cup is filled up with God's love, then it overflows to everyone around us. It's like rain that evaporates from the ocean to form clouds, then pours out as rain and snow to water the earth and make it flourish. This cycle of love compels us to love our spouses as Christ loves the church. We will speak healing words from our heart to our neighbors. Our children will know they are loved, disciplined and cared for because of our deepfelt, protective affections for them. This is the application of the Scripture that says, "If you love me, obey me."[4] The affections that were established in the first man come to life in new creations. On your own, this love is impossible. It is only possible in Christ.

Consider the heart of our heavenly Father. His thoughts turn to us so often that they are beyond our ability to count. How many grains of sand are there on the shore, on the bottom of the seas, and along the shorelines of lakes, rivers, and streams? More than all the sands of the earth are the thoughts of the Lord God toward each one of us. From His heart of love He calls out our name to come to Him so that He may hold us close to His heart. As He holds us to His heart, our own hearts will overflow to touch all those around us at home, at work, and in the community. We will become like a fountain that spills out Jesus' life-giving water.

This fountain that flows from our hearts is lifted up in worshipful service, and this is the way we love God from the heart: A cup of cold water offered to the thirsty. We give our jacket to a poor, shivering soul. The love that Abba Father floods into our hearts flows out to wash over all those who rub elbows with us every day.

This is love for our Lord God that flows from the heart.

How precious to me are your thoughts, God! How vast is the sum of them! Were I to count them, they would outnumber the grains of sand– when I awake, I am still with you.
(Psalm 139:17–18)

---

4. John 14:15.

6. Love the Lord with all Your Heart
Q & A

1. What is at the root of all the emotions that flow from the heart?

2. How are we brought into the full measure of God's love?

3. Is it even possible for fallible beings to love the Lord with our whole heart?

4. What is the effect of loving the Lord with all our heart?

My Journal Notes:

Chapter 7
Love the Lord with All Your Soul

This beautiful command has such rich depth in its purpose and intent. And, once again, the reality is that it's an impossible command if we attempt it on our own. This only becomes possible because He first loved us. Then we abound in this love in the Spirit, by whom we come into the fullness of Christ who loved us with the greatest love, even while we were still steeped in sin.[1] The first question we'll address in this study is: what is the soul? Then, we'll learn what the soul does and how it shapes our lives, our interactions, our work, our worship, and our love for our Lord God.

It's a challenge to study the soul because it is not like a body part we can hold up and describe. It can't be surgically removed and preserved to display before the class. Nor can it be illustrated. We'll learn what the soul is by describing its nature and effects. The soul becomes apparent by what it does and how it impacts us as a person. It's a different part of our being, unlike the spirit of a man or woman. Our spirit serves to lead body and soul into fellowship with the Holy Spirit. We worship in spirit[2] and our soul shapes our unique expressions of worship. This is an important study because we need to know what the soul is before we may love the Lord in the way He desires.[3]

The first soul came into existence as the Creator formed the man, Adam. The Holy Spirit breathed into him the breath of life and he became a living soul.[4] All who follow as Adam's progeny also have a soul. The soul may be the most intriguing part of a person, because it makes us who we are. Each person is as unique as our fingerprints, without equal because of our soul-print. We sing the way we do and speak with unique expressions because our soul gives us individuality. The soul shapes each person as an introvert or extrovert. If we like to work with our hands or prefer the realm of words as an academic—the soul influences our career preferences. This part of our being shapes the expressions of our heart. The soul determines the way we articulate ourselves; whether through song, written words, creative art, or speech patterns. This is all because of the penchant of our soul.

---

1. Romans 5:8.
2. John 4:24.
3. Cho Larson, "Body, Soul, and Spirit," Chap. 3 in *Treasures of the Kingdom*. Bloomington: WestBow Press, 2016.
4. Genesis 2:7.

> *These things I remember as I pour out my soul:*
> *how I used to go to the house of God under the protection of the*
> *Mighty One with shouts of joy and praise among the festive throng.*
> (Psalm 42:4)

The soul lends special flavor to our conversations and relationships. It shades and colors our interactions and reactions with family and friends. A writer's voice is unique according to the essence of her soul. An artist's creative bent rises up from the core of his being. A great orator's style of expression is like a fine wine poured out from the depths of her soul. From these examples we can see how important it is to love the Lord God with all our soul. All of who we are becomes a part of our unique expressions of love offered up to our heavenly Father in all that we do and say.

> *Praise the LORD, my soul; all my inmost being, praise his holy name.*
> *Praise the LORD, my soul, and forget not all his benefits.*
> (Psalm 103:1–2)

Life's deepest longings spring up from the depths of the soul.[5] A yearning for companionship, the desire for company around the dinner table, and the need to gather family around us on special occasions—all these desires come from the core of who we are as unique persons according to God's call on our life. It is from the wellsprings of these familial tugs that we love, honor, and yearn for our Lord God. In love from the soul, we come into agreement with all that the Father desires of us and for us, and our exaltations are received as an acceptable sacrifice with a sweet-smelling fragrance.

> *Let me go at once and assemble all Israel for my lord the king,*
> *so that they may make a covenant with you.*
> (2 Samuel 3:21)

Effective fasting and prayer are possible when there is agreement in our whole being. Bent knees and hearts lifted in prayer during a fast are best accomplished when body, soul, and spirit work together in agreement. This is a struggle because our flesh doesn't want to go without, even though our heart and soul desire what is right.[6] Our body will always complain that our knees hurt, but our soul connects with the strongest part of our being. Our soul is strengthened as it is led by our reborn spirit, or it's weakened by the desires of the flesh. It's important that they come together in agreement. This unity of purpose gives strength to our spirit to overrule and deny the weakness of the flesh so that we may step into the fullness of Christ as we fast and pray. The

---

5. Psalm 119:81.
6. Romans 8:5–7.

impulse to deny ourselves comes by the leading of the Spirit who breathes His desire into us, and then our soul is led to serve in its role in worshipful fasting and prayer.

> *Do two walk together unless they have agreed to do so?*
> (Amos 3:3)

When we get that empty sense deep down inside, this sentiment comes from the recesses of our soul. We serve an awesome God who loves us incredibly and will never leave us nor forsake us. And yet, there are times when it feels as if Abba Father steps back. These are times of testing to prove our love for Him. He may call us to examine our life and come to repentance before Him. In times like these, we're left with a sense that something is missing. That perception comes from the soul. This is a good time to listen to our soul's call and run to the Lord. The yearning of our soul drives us into His open arms where the Good Shepherd will reach out to us, restore our soul and fill us with His loving presence.

> *My soul yearns for you in the night; in the morning my spirit longs for you.*
> *When your judgments come upon the earth, the people of the world learn righteousness.*
> (Isaiah 26:9)

The Bridegroom's love for His bride is amazing to consider. We, the bride of Christ, are called to return His love in like manner, to the fullness of our being. What is so fascinating about God's love for His children is that He loves us the unique way He has made each of us—in a way that we each need to be loved as individuals. The Creator's love is not poured out in waves of generic love. It's as if the Almighty God blends special fragrances and flavors as love ingredients perfect for each one of us. In turn, it is from our distinct and special soul that we love the Father according to the way He has made us. Our voice and our unique way of expression shape these affections. There is no "one size fits all" love for our heavenly Father. The love language we use to express our affections toward the Father are determined by our soul. Because of this, the best fit for all who worship is to love the Lord God from the depths of our soul in the unique way that no one else can.

> *And they entered into a covenant to seek the LORD, the God of their fathers,*
> *with all their heart and with all their soul.*
> (2 Chronicles 15:12 ESV)

God loves each of us, teaches us, and disciplines us in a way that is perfect according to our soul. In a family, every child is distinct and special. Each one gives and receives love in different ways, just as they learn in various ways. It's as if each of us has customized expressions, desires, and affections. In a large family like the church, Abba Father shows his love in the best way each of us will receive it. Christ's love for the church is like a prayer blanket with tassels. It covers all of us and has a tassel for each of us.

Because He loves us, He disciplines us. This discipline is custom-designed to be most effective for our individual needs, and to show us God's glory in a way we can see. Because of this, when we love our Lord God, when the Holy Spirit admonishes us, and when we are disciplined, a righteous, repentant response wells up from our soul.

> *But what can I say? He has spoken to me, and he himself has done this. I will walk humbly all my years because of this anguish of my soul.*
> (Isaiah 38:15)

Early Christians were often faced with a choice: to deny Christ or be thrown into the arena with ravenous lions. Since then, more Christians than we can count have been martyred for their faith. Persecution of Christians in the 21st Century has hit that exponential curve with rapidly increasing violence against all those who are in Christ. As we near the end of the age, the church will become the scapegoat for everything that goes wrong in the world. Many religious zealots will react with increased violence against God's people. One of the most infamous historic persecutions occurred in the Ottoman Empire when Anti-Christian pogroms inflicted widespread massacres. Over 325,000 Christians were slaughtered and another 546,000 driven from their homes and deported. This is minuscule compared to what is to come as we approach the day of the Lord.

But even the greatest violence inflicted against God's people cannot and will not defeat them. What lasting harm can the violent inflict upon Christ's followers? The violent can kill the body, but they cannot destroy a person's eternal soul and spirit. In fact, giving up our life for Christ and the cross of Christ makes us one with Jesus. Jesus' sacrifice is more powerful than the bullet that takes our life. This is the reason we lift up our souls to the One who preserves us so we may spend an eternity with Him.

> *Do not be afraid of those who kill the body but cannot kill the soul. Rather, be afraid of the One who can destroy both soul and body in hell.*
> (Matthew 10:28)

The soul was never intended to serve as the dominant part of our being. It's always best when our redeemed spirit is in Christ and rules over soul and body. When the soul attempts to rule, our worship becomes soulish, rather than selfless. This means that our worship serves to satisfy our whims.

Instead, we are called to lift up and adore the Lord God from the whole of our being. When our spirit is submitted to Christ, strengthened in the Word, and led by the Holy Spirit, it is prepared to rule over our soul and body with great benefits for the whole of our lives.

> *Dear friend, I pray that you may enjoy good health and that*
> *all may go well with you, even as your soul is getting along well.*
> (3 John 1:2)

Life is a constant struggle. We gain a little and it's persistently grabbed away through difficult circumstances beyond our control. We struggle to step up one rung of the ladder, then we're knocked down a couple rungs. But in Christ we find an ever-present help. In the shadow of His wings we find a peaceful place to breathe in safety. Our stressed soul is restored and redirected in spite of every wrong turn in the past. We may feel like a lamb attacked by a lion, but the Good Shepherd rescues us from the jaws of death. Now we're in the safety of His arms and from the inner core of who we are we can lift up our soul to rejoice to the Lord.

> *Then my soul will rejoice in the LORD and delight in his salvation.*
> *My whole being will exclaim, "Who is like you, LORD?*
> *You rescue the poor from those too strong for them,*
> *the poor and needy from those who rob them."*
> (Psalm 35:9–10)

When our voices are raised up with delight and our whole beings are lifted up to exclaim the joy of the Lord, all this is made possible because the strength of our soul joins together with our spirit. Mary, mother of Jesus, offers us a beautiful example of the power of this union as she breaks out in prophetic song. She sings melodious words with eternal impact. Mary's heart delights and her soul rejoices to exclaim her joy in the Lord. Her whole person joins with the Holy Spirit to exalt the Lord for the abundance of His saving grace. She glorified God who humbled her to serve as a vessel so that His power would be manifested to save all who will come and receive.

> *And Mary said: "My soul glorifies the Lord and my spirit rejoices in God my Savior,*
> *for he has been mindful of the humble state of his servant.*
> *From now on all generations will call me blessed,*
> *for the Mighty One has done great things for me–holy is his name."*
> (Luke 1:46–49)

The command to love is a beautiful imperative. Obeying this command brings us into a soulful kind of love that binds us together in a covenant relationship overflowing with blessings. This love is individually unique in both the way our Father God loves us, and in the manner we express this love in return. The Father's affections cover and enfold all of us with wings for each of us to receive and express love. The way we love our heavenly Father and then overflow with that same love is shaped by each individual's soul. God's affections toward us compel us to gather together and worship as one in Christ. Corporate worship is like mixing the best varieties of wine together to make one great joy-filled cup to lift up before the Lord.

How could we want any less than to love the Lord with all our soul, and from the deepest recesses of our soul?

The king stood by the pillar and renewed the covenant in the presence of the LORD– to follow the LORD and keep his commands, statutes and decrees with all his heart and all his soul, thus confirming the words of the covenant written in this book. Then all the people pledged themselves to the covenant.
(2 Kings 23:3)

7. Love the Lord with all Your Soul
Q & A

1. Why is our soul the most intriguing and unique part of who we are?

2. Why is it so important to love God with all our soul?

3. What part does the soul have in true and real worship?

4. Describe how Father God's love for each individual is unique and special.

5. What part does the soul serve in our three-part beings—body, soul, and spirit?

My Journal Notes:

Chapter 8
Love the Lord with all Your Mind

Key Scriptures:

- "The end of all things is near. Therefore be alert and of sober mind so that you may pray." (1 Peter 4:7)
- "Finally, brothers and sisters, rejoice! Strive for full restoration, encourage one another, be of one mind, live in peace. And the God of love and peace will be with you." (2 Corinthians 13:11)

This session will help to direct our thoughts toward the kingdom of heaven. We will learn about the mind as an important part of loving our Lord God with all of who we are. Love is our purpose, and the mind is a crucial partner in expressing our affections toward the Lord Almighty. The mind is not above all else because, if our love for the Lord God is only intellectual, our love is incomplete.

Christianity is not a religion that requires us to leave our mind on the shelf as we enter. The thought processes of a disciple of Jesus are an important part of their whole person as they come to love the Creator of all heaven and earth. We need a sharp mind so the Spirit of Christ can impart knowledge and good judgment to us.[1] Intellectual honesty allows us to get a clear picture of the wisdom that is taught in the Bible. Our thoughts play a crucial role as we comprehend, receive, and express the Father's love. With our minds, we think to cherish our heavenly Father because of His abundant goodness to us. When we ponder His blessings, it helps us to think and take a personal account of ourselves in light of God's goodness toward us. Meditating on the Scriptures and acting upon what we learn is accomplished as mind, soul, and spirit work together to keep us on the right path.[2] Our thought processes play an active role as we chew and digest these truths of the Word.

The mind takes in what the ears hear so we may comprehend the Scriptures and come to know the beauty and majesty of our Lord and Savior. This knowledge of God's love is a stepping stone toward unshakeable faith. The intellect helps us to prepare the fallow ground[3] for the seed of faith to be planted in our hearts. Some of our minds work like Thomas', who doubted Christ's resurrection until he could see Jesus' pierced hands and touch His pierced side. When his eyes saw the evidence of the crucifixion on Jesus' body, this satisfied

---
1. Psalm 119:66.
2. Psalm 119:104.
3. Hosea 10:12.

his mind and his spirit could believe and embrace the resurrected Christ.

> *But he* [Thomas] *said to them, "Unless I see the nail marks in his hands and put my finger where the nails were, and put my hand into his side, I will not believe." A week later his disciples were in the house again, and Thomas was with them. Though the doors were locked, Jesus came and stood among them and said, "Peace be with you!" Then he said to Thomas, "Put your finger here; see my hands. Reach out your hand and put it into my side. Stop doubting and believe." Thomas said to him, "My Lord and my God!" Then Jesus told him, "Because you have seen me, you have believed; blessed are those who have not seen and yet have believed."*
> (John 20:25–29)

All our minds work in special ways and there are many good reasons to celebrate our differences. Some people come to saving faith because of the Spirit's impulse in their hearts when they hear and comprehend the truths of the Gospel. Many people hear God's commands and, for the first time, see their sinful condition. God's precepts cause them to grieve over their sin, confess their sin, and come to Christ Jesus for forgiveness and saving grace. Others come to faith when the warmth of a special friendship opens their minds to hear the message of the Gospel. For some, they must understand what they hear and place it side by side with convincing proofs, and this opens the door to faith. A lot of thoughtful people take a mental account of the truths of the kingdom of heaven by examining the actions of those who have already come to believe. Some need to see documentation of the physical evidence of Biblical history before they will open their minds to hear the truths of the Scripture.

As an example: Luke, the physician, wrote his Gospel to "most excellent Theophilus, so that you may know the certainty of the things you have been taught."[4] Apparently, Theophilus needed to read the eyewitness accounts that Luke compiled to strengthen his faith.

Our minds are all wired a little different and the Holy Spirit connects with us according to our personal diagram. Our intellect is one threshold to cross before we will hear, receive, and believe the truths of this great salvation. Every one of us, with our own unique ways of thinking, ought to use our mental capacity to do the work God has provided, to serve our family and neighbors, and to love our heavenly Father. The prophet Isaiah gives us a beautiful illustration of how God teaches us and deals with us according to the unique way He has shaped each one of us:

---

4. Luke 1:3–4.

> *When a farmer plows for planting, does he plow continually? Does he keep on breaking up and working the soil? When he has leveled the surface, does he not sow caraway and scatter cumin? Does he not plant wheat in its place, barley in its plot, and spelt in its field? His God instructs him and teaches him the right way. Caraway is not threshed with a sledge, nor is the wheel of a cart rolled over cumin; caraway is beaten out with a rod, and cumin with a stick. Grain must be ground to make bread; so one does not go on threshing it forever. The wheels of a threshing cart may be rolled over it, but one does not use horses to grind grain. All this also comes from the LORD Almighty, whose plan is wonderful, whose wisdom is magnificent.*
> (Isaiah 28:24–29)

As we consider the mind, a word of caution is necessary. If belief gets stuck in our intellect and goes no further, the roots of faith will be too shallow to survive. A teacher can give instructions and information for the mind to absorb, but this is only a good foundation. The mind can be catechized with principles of Christian religion to prepare the student to answer questions, but the effect of those words must not stop there. Scriptures heard with the ears and seeded in the mind must be received and believed as if they wash over us and soak into our body, soul, and spirit. Intellectual assent to the reality of God's existence, the truth of the Bible, and the words of the Gospel is no more than a good step. Intellectual acceptance alone is not the means of saving faith. The power of the Word and the Holy Spirit work to transform hardened hearts and willful minds.

> *The seed falling among the thorns refers to someone who hears the word, but the worries of this life and the deceitfulness of wealth choke the word, making it unfruitful.*
> (Matthew 13:22)

The mind can also serve to distract us from entering into God's rest by faith alone. Some of us carry baggage from the junk we've fed our mind in the past and this rubbish has created barriers in our mind. This is the reason renewing our minds is so important. Our thought processes, our imaginations, and the things that pop into our minds must constantly be cast upon the Lord who forgives us and cleanses us from all unrighteousness. Our depraved thoughts must be taken captive in Christ. A polluted mind is one of many serious distractions Christ Jesus overcomes in us.

As an example: we miss the truth, power, and reality of baptism if we are baptized only because we made note of points presented in class and see the process as connecting those dots. If we simply complete the checklist so we can get a baptismal certificate, all we have is a useless piece of paper.

A baptism that is little more than a well instructed religious obligation becomes a man-made ceremony. Understand that while baptism must not be limited to the intellect, the mind serves a crucial role in knowing the power and purpose of true baptism.

This is important because an earthbound mind will work to harden our hearts and draw us away from Christ. Intellectual duplicity causes us to twist truth with selective hearing—taking in only what pleases us. Our inmost thoughts can become strongholds of pride.[5] It's the mind that leads us to worry about life's problems and gets us worked up about losing the material things we treasure too much. A mind set on the treasures of this world will set our feet in the wrong direction. We will become like the man Jesus invited to sell everything. He needed to get rid of his baggage by giving it to the poor before he could follow Jesus.

> *When the young man heard this, he went away sad, because he had great wealth.*
> (Matthew 19:22)

Why would anyone allow life's possessions to create a stronghold in their minds? But we are all vulnerable to this materialistic trap. Instead, when we purchase something, we should consider that it's not ours to keep.[6] The death grip we have on earthbound assets must be broken because they steal us away from our Lord and Savior.

How could we let these possessions influence us to reject a heaven-sent love that is greater than any human capacity can ever comprehend? This love is abundant, all encompassing, goes further, accomplishes more, and its impact is wider than human knowledge can grasp. It is so infinite we may take an eternity to learn the vast dimensions of God's love. In God's final glory, our regenerated minds will be opened to learn the riches of God's eternal kingdom and this blessed quest may take forever. But today, when we teach Christ's passion-driven love, preach sermons, teach Bible studies, and even watch movies that reenact His crucifixion, the full extent of Jesus' love is way beyond our ability to grasp. Even so, when we put life's baggage aside and seek to know Christ's love, it's a delightful pursuit.

> *To know this love that surpasses knowledge–*
> *that you may be filled to the measure of all the fullness of God.*
> (Ephesians 3:19)

Loving the Lord our God requires the whole of our person to be involved. Our whole heart, energies, ambitions, personalities, and an intellectually

---

5. Luke 1:51, Colossians 2:18.
6. 1 Corinthians 7:30.

honest mind are necessary. When we lift up our hands to heaven, our voice in songs of exaltation, and our spirit to exalt the Lord in jubilant worship; in all this the mind serves a crucial part. A clear head is needed to learn God's commands. God's word stirs our mind so that we may be taught His decrees.[7] A Scripture-bathed mentality serves to direct our energies into serving and our ambitions toward the kingdom of heaven. A regenerated mind helps us to voice praises to God Almighty. Let these good things be the focus of our minds so that life's pitfalls are never allowed to keep us from pursuing insights of God's kingdom.

So I turned my mind to understand, to investigate and to search out wisdom and the scheme of things and to understand the stupidity of wickedness and the madness of folly.
(Ecclesiastes 7:25)

The mind performs a critical role in helping us to walk in accord with God's precepts. An obedient walk makes our love for the Father evident. The Bible was written for us to read with Spirit-inspired understanding, because only the Spirit who inspired the Scriptures can open and instruct our minds with regard to the truths of God's word. Sensible thought processes are part of learning as we are taught the holy Scriptures, and this leads us to see our need of Christ. But when we confine ourselves to our own mental abilities, our capacity to understand the truths of the kingdom is limited. A teachable spirit joins together with a well-instructed mind to great effect.

Test me, LORD, and try me, examine my heart and my mind.
(Psalm 26:2)

The intellect needs to come into agreement with soul and spirit because every part of us is called to love the Lord God. Our thought processes help us to weigh ourselves in light of the Scriptures to know our strengths, our needs, our weaknesses, and our vulnerabilities. When we take account of ourselves, it helps to resist the temptations that come against us. Our renewed mind, in agreement with our restored soul and refreshed spirit, makes for a tough line of defense to break through. When we work together, there is strength to bear up against snares and temptations. But, when an earthbound mind rules, we become closed to the truths of the Gospel and vulnerable to the world's temptations.

No temptation has overtaken you except what is common to mankind.
And God is faithful; he will not let you be tempted beyond what you can bear.
But when you are tempted, he will also provide a way out so that you can endure it.
(1 Corinthians 10:13)

---
7. Psalm 119:71.

We are instructed to have the mind of Christ. When we become new creations in Christ, this includes our intellect as well.[8] Our renewed mind keeps us on track with the Lord Jesus. When we are baptized into Christ, that means every part of us is baptized. With minds bathed in Christ, it becomes a delight to search out the valuable treasures of the kingdom of heaven.

The Apostle Paul wrote to the Philippian church instructing them to let the mind of Christ be an integral part of who they were. He offered himself as an example. He came to them with the most precious pearls of wisdom from the kingdom of heaven spoken in plain spiritual words. He could say these things because he discarded all beliefs founded in human wisdom.[9] Hearing ears and a restored mind open our eyes to see Christ unveiled in many Old Testament types. The lives the patriarchs lived make the counsels of God clear and unlock the mysteries of the kingdom of heaven. There is no natural power, no human reasoning, no genius intellect that can make known the mind of God.

> *And you, my son Solomon, acknowledge the God of your father, and serve him with wholehearted devotion and with a willing mind, for the LORD searches every heart and understands every desire and every thought.*
> *(1 Chronicles 28:9)*

Loving the Lord our God is an intelligent, reasoned, and sensible kind of love. And yet, our mindful affections are only one rung on the whole ladder. A great way to step up to a greater love is to study, meditate, and understand the Creator as He has revealed Himself in the Scriptures. The Word of Creation makes Himself known in holy words that plant seeds of faith in our hearts. His words are gifts filled with wisdom and insight that empower us to love the Lord God with all our heart, soul, mind, and spirit.

When we gain knowledge of the imperatives in the Bible, our feet have light to follow the right pathway. Our footprints on this path of obedience are evidence of our love.[10] The light of the Scriptures keeps our feet from every wrong path. To gain insights of Christ is to find stepping stones that lead us into delighted obedience, and the love of our Lord and Savior will flood over us and through us.

The human mind can be taught about all these good things, but if it is no more than learned information, a list of stuff we must do or must not do, we have a very impoverished kind of Christianity. We can write volumes of notes from our Bible classes about God's love and still only know *about* God's love.

---

8. 2 Corinthians 5:17.
9. Philippians 3:8.
10. John 14:15.

The full knowledge of God's love comes through the power of the word and the ministries of the Spirit of Christ.

Every human mind is unique and special, and our heavenly Father comes to us with a personal love that fits us like a custom-made glove. Even though our mind will never completely understand how great His affections are toward us, our intellect takes part along with heart and soul to express love for our heavenly Father. When our entire being comes together in agreement, with nothing held back, this is a significant step toward worshipping the Creator of all heaven and earth in spirit and truth.

8. Love the Lord with all Your Mind
Q & A

1. What part does our mind play in comprehending God's immeasurable love?

2. Describe the intellectual threshold that often must be crossed to know God's love.

3. What happens if belief ends as no more than an intellectual assent to the reality of Creator God, the Bible, and Jesus Christ?

4. How does a renewed mind serve to help us walk in delighted obedience?

My Journal Notes:

Chapter 9
Love Your Neighbor as Yourself

Key Scriptures:

- "[Elizabeth's] neighbors and relatives heard that the Lord had shown her great mercy, and they shared her joy." (Luke 1:58)
- "He asked Jesus, 'And who is my neighbor?'" (Luke 10:29)

Perilous times bring out the best and the worst in people. The cries of the destitute overwhelm us like tidal waves when disasters mess up our normal. Those left standing get flooded with pleas from the desperate. But people's responses vary dramatically. Predators loot and prey on the weak in times like this. Robber barons wring out extra profits. Those in authority grab for more power. And a few super-rich tech giants give from their wealth to advance their cause. The proud and powerful kick the victim to the side of the road as an unsightly disturbance, an insult to the senses, or exploit them as an opportunity for gain.

On the other side of the coin, simple folks lift up the poor and give out of their humble means. A person shivering outside the grocery store gets a coat wrapped around their shoulders. A stranded mother is offered a ride home, and her empty cupboards get restocked. The assistance we offer is personal and often close to home.

In this study, we'll consider the ways that we love and care for ourselves and how that relates to loving our neighbor in the same way. Close and personal examples will help us apply Jesus' teaching to everyday living. Not everyone is called to pack up and go to Tanzania, live in a grass hut, and eat fire roasted bugs for breakfast, lunch, and dinner. Most often our neighbors are much closer to home.

For both powerful and humble people, the injured man lying unconscious at the side of the road tests their sensibilities, and what is in their heart will pour out. If greed fills their heart, they'll rifle through his pockets for anything of value. Hearts filled with generosity will get out the first-aid kit and get to work. A self-indulgent heart jealously ignores a neighbor's good fortune, but a generous heart brings the champaign to celebrate. When Christ's love fills a heart, neighborly love spurs us to act.

To the humble, a poor victim lying at the side of the road is a neighbor in need and they give of their limited means to help. Jesus' parabolic image of a man who lays injured on the side of the road, a victim of robbers, teaches us how to identify our neighbor—anyone we see who is in need.

The essence of this foundational command gets down to the nitty-gritty of life. This is where theology meets reality. When we live by this truth, the narrow pathway meets life in the trenches. It's like we walk on heaven's path while reaching out to lift up those who are caught in the grips of darkness and despair.

In real world moments like this, it's good to ask: "How do we love ourselves?" as we venture to help our neighbor. When we learn how to love and care for our own well-being, we can see why it's important to love our neighbor in the same way.

Consider these real-life examples of loving ourselves to see how this helps us to love our neighbor in like manner:

We exercise to strengthen our bodies, but a buff body isn't our primary purpose. Our aim is a fit, breathing, functioning body to keep us here on terra firma for a while longer. A healthy body is important so we can work to provide for our families. We need strength to teach and play with our kids and grandkids. Because of these needs, and because we care about ourselves, we exercise to strengthen our bodies. We live as examples to encourage those around us to keep themselves as healthy and strong as possible. Maybe the little girl down the street needs a bicycle with training wheels so she can get out of the house and ride with the neighbor kids. Another neighbor may need the helmet our child grew out of to keep her child safe on his scooter. We love ourselves enough to keep healthy, and in the same way we consider others' needs for their health and well-being.

For physical training is of some value, but godliness [spiritual training] *is of value in everything and in every way, since it holds promise for the present life and for the life to come.*
(1 Timothy 4:8)

When we really care about ourselves, we listen to what our body needs. We Google our symptoms and, after the panic subsides, we settle down and simply change our diet. If our condition is serious enough, we make a doctor appointment. When our back muscles scream at us, the physical therapist adds a stretching exercise to our morning routine. Our body's signals are worth listening to and, because we care about ourselves, we act to take care of what our body needs.

With the same concern, we are called to listen to our neighbor. We listen with empathy when they try to figure out what causes their persistent headaches. A shoulder rub may be the perfect fix. A sympathetic ear could be the best cure anyone could offer. A chance to laugh at corny jokes could be the perfect medicine. When we take time to converse, this proves we care for them. A show of concern and help finding resources are good and helpful ways to serve. The way we care for our own health is a good life habit that will encourage and help those around us to care for themselves.

When winter is just around the corner and the Farmer's Almanac predicts some serious polar storms in our region, we're prompted to go to the coat closet and take an inventory of our winter clothes. Our rain jacket is worn a bit thin, and last year we gave away our winter parka to a friend who got laid off at work. The results of this inventory inspire us to check our budget and start shopping for new winter duds because we don't want our family to shiver through the cold spells. Icicles are nice on the edge of the roof but not on the nose.

Our neighbor has many of the same needs as we do and, because of this, we can keep an eye out for the ones who have few resources. We can whisper a prayer and then ask them, "Do your kids have winter shoes and coats?" And, if not, ask what we can do to help them get what they need.

We prepare ourselves and our family for a long winter chill, and look out for our neighbor who will have to face the same winter storms.

He [a godly person] *gives his food to the hungry and provides clothing for the naked.* (Ezekiel 18:16)

We have all stubbed our toe on a chair. Our morning started great. We danced a jig around the dining room table. We sang a silly tune while carrying our jogging shoes to get ready for a morning run, but then we stubbed our toe. Now we're using an ice pack and there's no way we can run—our toe hurts too much. We limp across the room to get our cell phone; maybe we should call in sick. How can we jump in and out of our delivery truck all day when we can hardly walk? But it's only our big toe that hurts, right? There's nothing wrong with the rest of our body. So why do we feel all crippled up? Is it possible that one little appendage can put our whole body in a big hurt?

The Apostle Paul uses a similar illustration to teach that we are parts of a whole. We're part of a family, neighborhood, society, and especially a vital, functioning part of a community of Christian faith. From Paul's letters, we come to understand that when one person in a group suffers, we all suffer with them, or possibly because of them. We see examples of this in professional life. When a few lawyers turn rotten, the whole profession gets a bad rap. When some contractors build shoddy houses, all building trades to get a black eye. This reality is amplified in the church. The few pastors who get caught up in moral failures stain the whole church, cause all Christians to be scorned, and Jesus' holy name is tarnished.

When one small part of our community hurts it affects the whole. For this reason, it's important for everyone to consider others to see how we can strengthen all those around us. Take care of the bruised toe, and the whole body will benefit.

> *If one part suffers, every part suffers with it; if one part is honored,*
> *every part rejoices with it.*
> (1 Corinthians 12:26)

One of the great benefits of turning the calendar to a New Year is that we have an opportunity to start over. We get a fresh start on taking care of ourselves. The Grim Reaper is forgotten and it's like we're given a new baby to nurture and nourish. Those extra pounds we gained from Grandma's pumpkin pie and Dad's special apfelstrudel need to come off. January 2nd is self-improvement time. And finally, when springtime rolls around and the scale stops at the right number, we reward ourselves with new running shoes.

We have learned to take care of ourselves and improve our life because we like who we are and where our life is leading us. It's good to look out for others with the same fervor, and the best place to start is right at home. For instance, we raise our children in a way that is best suited for them. We get to know their personalities, gifts, and what they like and don't like. Based on firsthand observation, we encourage our children to advance in their talents and tastes. If they're an artist, we encourage them by providing paint, paper, and guidance. We turn on the music for the child who constantly dances and they're given the opportunity for dance lessons after we save up. It's even better when our inclination for encouragement spills over to our child's friends who come over to play. We can recognize and encourage them and their parents as the opportunity presents itself.

We work toward our life goals and career aspirations because we're happy with the person that God has made us. In the same way, we bless and encourage those around us, especially those right in our own home.

> *Start children off on the way they should go,*
> *and even when they are old they will not turn from it.*
> (Proverbs 22:6)

Comparing ourselves to other people is a self-destructive exercise. Instead, the best thing we can do is to consider where we started and how far we've come. But when we compare ourselves with others, we tend to look for people with whom we compare favorably. We want to look better than those people on the other side of town. Our new SUV with a prestigious logo on the steering wheel makes us feel better about ourselves, especially when the guy on the other side of the street drives an old Ford sedan with peeling paint.

But we've got it all backwards. Our vaunted efforts to exalt ourselves are a formula for personal failure. This truth became painfully evident when Jesus was nailed to die on a Roman cross. All but one of His disciples fled from the danger. The men disappeared who once scrambled to better their standing with Jesus. The guys vanished who once yearned for positions of power in the kingdom they thought Jesus would establish in the nation of Israel. But who was found faithful? Who would remain and boldly stand there at the foot of the cross to grieve as Jesus died? Who were the first to take incense to Jesus' grave? The women who followed Jesus to serve His needs were the same ones who stuck with Him to the end. They, like Jesus, had hearts of servants and they were honored as the first witnesses of the resurrected Christ.

John was the only disciple who stood beside Mary, mother of Jesus, Mary, mother of James and Joses, Salome, Mary Magdalene, and Martha. They had the mind of Christ—a mind to serve. They considered others better than themselves and, because of this, they followed Jesus right up to the fulfillment of His passion on a hill called Golgotha. The women who stood at the foot of Jesus' cross made it their ambition to attend to other's needs. The longing of Jesus' heart was their greatest concern even as they stood at the foot of the cross.

We ought to emulate them. It's good when we appreciate ourselves just the way God made us and then esteem others as better than ourselves. This is the attitude, mindset, and perspective of a servant who faithfully serves at the foot of the cross.

Do nothing out of selfish ambition or vain conceit.
Rather, in humility value others above yourselves,
not looking to your own interests but each of you to the interests of the others.
(Philippians 2:3–4)

Reliable, honest, and diligent workers are crucial to the success of any small business. An entrepreneur's livelihood, making payroll, and paying the rent all depend on cohesive associates who work together to meet customer expectations. Purpose-driven teams typically consist of a leader and qualified members who use their talents for the good of everyone concerned. This same concept is an important part of caring for our neighbors.

If the boss sets himself up as the biggest cheese and pushes the workers into subservient positions to perform at his command, he may succeed for a while, but he has essentially sealed his doom. When a proprietor takes advantage of his workers or cheats them out of their pay, the Good Lord knows and will deal with him accordingly in due time.

This truth works both ways. What a supervisor does will come back to haunt or to bless him. Likewise, what the workers do for the good or harm of the business and customers will either return to bless or destroy the whole team and enterprise. Both boss and worker should consider what it's like to walk in the other's shoes and adjust their attitude toward work accordingly. It's simply the neighborly thing to do.

> *Serve wholeheartedly, as if you were serving the Lord, not people, because you know that the Lord will reward each one for whatever good they do, whether they are slave or free. And masters, treat your slaves in the same way. Do not threaten them, since you know that he who is both their Master and yours is in heaven, and there is no favoritism with him.*
> (Ephesians 6:7–10)

If you're ever asked to judge an art show, be careful as you consider your answer. It's a perilous task. Various mediums of art are splashed on canvas, shaped into clay vessels, snapped with a camera lens, or cast in bronze. Every expression comes from deep-felt emotions that flow out of the maker's heart and soul. Judging another person's work is a complicated task, and one that must be accepted with the right attitude.

But what if your own work of art is included in the show? You know perfectly well about your racing thoughts, the emotions expressed, and the challenges faced while creating your masterpiece. Everything that went wrong in the process is evident only to you—and, in spite of the challenges, you overcame the obstacles and created the most beautiful painting ever. Or so you think. Because of this blind spot you excuse the slight imperfections in your work. In fact, it's as if you have a log in your eye when it comes to judging your own work alongside others who couldn't possibly have overcome the obstacles you conquered. And when you see the imperfections in their work of art, it's easy to think it's because of their lack of experience, poor skills, or just plain sloppiness.

A better way is to judge your own work first and consider your flaws, fallibilities, weaknesses, and failings. Then, with a contrite attitude, be honest about your failings so you can overcome them.

Now you're ready to be a neighborly kind of judge who understands that every artist has challenges, and you can encourage them in their talents to win an award in this show or in the next. Judge yourself first and then, with clear eyes, consider your neighbor's plight with the same mercy you showed yourself. The Best of Show award will go to the most deserving soul.

> *First take the plank out of your own eye, and then you will see clearly*
> *to remove the speck from your brother's eye.*
> (Matthew 7:5)

After a long and flattering introduction, the speaker made his way to the podium with notes scrunched in his sweaty hands. He leaned into the microphone and said, "I don't deserve any of those great accolades, but then, I don't deserve to be bald either." Flattery is one of the most manipulative ways to assault a person. We are all suckers for flattery. We want to hear good things about ourselves. We want to know that other people think good things about us.

But flattery is often a trap. It's not a neighborly thing to do. People can see our need to know that we're a good person, and then use flattering words to gain favor and get what they want from us.

Flattery is different from a compliment. A compliment expresses a genuine appreciation of something specific we have accomplished. We all know how flattery works. When we want a favor from someone who may be reluctant, we just tell them how beautiful and wonderful they are. It's a trap that is all too effective, but he who flatters will fall into his own trap.[1] Flattery is insincere praise, often thrown out like bait to achieve a selfish purpose. If we really care about a person, we'll recognize them and their achievements with a gracious comment to encourage them.

If our concern for our friend and neighbor is real, we don't flatter them because it might trip them up. We don't want our neighbor to rave about our green thumb only because they want to pick raspberries in our garden. In the same way, we don't praise our neighbor for the beautiful apple crop she raised this year so she'll give us enough apples to bake a pie.

> *Those who flatter their neighbors are spreading nets for their feet.*
> (Proverbs 29:5)

Loving our neighbor as ourselves is where this walk of faith meets real life. We love and care for ourselves so we can serve our neighbor in her time of need. But who is our neighbor? Is it the family next door? Are mountain villagers in Colombia our neighbors? Of course they are. Our neighbors are both close to home and in other parts of the world. And we meet their needs in the same way we would want them to help us in our time of trouble.

We exercise to keep strong and healthy so we can care for others. We care for ourselves and then in the same way we love and care for our neighbor. We do this because the love of Christ is at work in us and through us. This is im-

---
1. Proverbs 28:10.

portant because one person's weakness, one neighbor's lack, has an effect on everybody around them. Our first duty is to take care of ourselves, our family, and to treat our neighbors the same way we want them to treat us.

9. Love Your Neighbor as Yourself
Q & A

1. Why do people react so differently to the disasters happening around them?

2. When Christ's love fills our hearts, how will this affect the way we respond to a neighbor in need?

3. How does loving ourselves help us to love our neighbors?

4. When a family hurts and is in need, how does this affect the whole community?

My Journal Notes:

Chapter 10
Love Your Enemies

Key Scriptures:

- "But to you who are listening I say: Love your enemies, do good to those who hate you, bless those who curse you, pray for those who mistreat you." (Luke 6:27–28)
- "Then he [Stephen] fell on his knees and cried out, 'Lord, do not hold this sin against them.' When he had said this, he fell asleep." (Acts 7:60)

"Love our enemies? You gotta be kidding!"

Jesus' command to love our enemies is contrary to human nature. In this study, we'll learn that it's only possible in a right-side up kingdom. Christ's kingdom is such a realm. Jesus doesn't teach us to lay down and let people walk on us. That's not love for ourselves or anyone else. His command to love our enemies is not a call to submit to abuse. Turning the other cheek after being struck in the face isn't a call for us to invite further violence. In essence, Jesus teaches us to love ourselves and not to allow abuse or reciprocate with abuse. His message teaches us not to hit back at the person who strikes us. We are not to insult those who insult us. These concepts are the essence of this study session.

We've all heard people say, "I don't get mad, I get even." That's not a good plan. The kingdom's pathway shows us a better way. Get angry? Certainly! But it should be constructive anger that helps to achieve what is right. We cast our cares, our anger, and our frustrations on the Lord because He cares for us. Tell the Father you're angry about what happened to you, and then leave the offender's consequences in the Lord's hands. You can be sure that God is more than able to avenge the wrong.

The Bible teaches us to cast our burdens on Him.[1] This includes the times we're offended and angry. We must cast our cares on the Father because vengeance belongs to Him.[2] God provides the appointed authorities to protect us and deal with the offender according to law and justice. The street cop and first responder are, in fact, God ordained servants.[3] But what can we do when the system fails and rules in favor of injustice rather than justice? We must appeal to the highest court, the Judge of all heaven and earth. We never take matters into our own hands. Rest in the fact that God will hear and will always do what is best on our behalf.

---
1. 1 Peter 5:7.
2. Deuteronomy 32:35, Romans 12:19.
3. Romans 13:1.

Jesus' teachings are as countercultural as it gets, and His message is clear. If someone sues us to take our coat, give them our shirt too. If we're forced to pack a man's backpack for a mile, carry it two miles in Jesus' name. We are called to love even those who couldn't care less about us. To lend a family money to pay their rent even if we know they'll never pay us back. Has someone treated us unmercifully? Show them mercy.

What will you do when you're driving along in the middle lane, close to the speed limit, minding your own business, and some guy almost clips your front fender trying to cut you off? It will make you fume. You'll want to step on the gas to show him you're no milquetoast. Showing him some sign language may occur to you, but you know it's best to resist these temptations and continue safely on your way to work.

Then, a mile or two down the road, there his car sits with a flat tire and he signals for help. Will you stop to help him? What if you see him at the side of the road with a patrol car behind him? Will you laugh at your neighbor?[4]

> *If you see the donkey of someone who hates you fallen down under its load, do not leave it there; be sure you help them with it.*
> (Exodus 23:5)

When we feel offended and hurt, the last thing on our minds is to help the person who caused us harm. Then, about the time we think we've finally got over the pain of it and begin to entertain kind and forgiving thoughts toward the offender—they do it again. It can become a vicious emotional circus as we try to deal with odious people. But the mind of Christ directs our thoughts to serve those around us. In reality, this kind of service is humanly impossible, but it is made possible for all who are in Christ.

Must we repress our anger, our hurt, and our frustrations? Do we just swallow that bitter pill that feels like a big lump in our throat? Not at all. Jesus is our Counselor and He has given us the Holy Spirit as Comforter. He invites us to pour out to Him the bitterness of our soul.[5] We can weep with angry tears and let our hearts cry out to Him. We can talk in confidence with a close friend who will stand with us as we grieve for what has been stolen away.

Then, after we have cast our burdens upon the Lord, the weights of these offenses lift from our shoulders and we're finally able to let go and forgive. We feed our enemy the bread of forgiveness. We offer living water even to that cruel and angry person who becomes thirsty. Our heavenly Father can change the heart of the person who harmed us and He will heal our deepest

---

4. Proverbs 24:17.
5. Ephesians 4:31.

wounds. When the healing is complete, we may find ourselves ready to invite them to join us at a table of plenty: plenty of food, plenty of refreshments, and plenty of mercy and forgiveness.

> *If your enemy is hungry, give him food to eat;*
> *if he is thirsty, give him water to drink.*
> (Proverbs 25:21)

The law of love is written on the hearts of all God's sons and daughters; simple and clear precepts written in indelible ink. This law guides our convictions, desires, passions, zeal, and actions. What is written on our hearts compels us to apply the Golden Rule to every part of our lives and interactions with family, friends, neighbors, and coworkers. We must not allow this perfect law to become confused or corrupted by a hardened and rebellious heart. The Old Testament law provides commandments for living, and now the law of love calls us to a higher standard.[6] This standard is the measure we apply in all that we do for those around us.

> *So in everything, do to others what you would have them do to you,*
> *for this sums up the Law and the Prophets.*
> (Matthew 7:12)

The desire of our hearts ought to be a love that is quick to forgive even in a moment of serious suffering. Our natural tendency is to lash out with harsh words, or attempt to get even. But in the strength of the Spirit and the Word, we can overrule these natural inclinations. Even before the suffering is over, our hearts are ready with an attitude of forgiveness and mercy.

After being falsely accused, beaten beyond recognition, spit upon, mocked, His beard torn out, a crown of thorns pressed on His head, His back torn open with a whip, and then nailed to a rugged wooden cross to suffer and die, Jesus called out to the Father to forgive His enemies because of their ignorance:

> *Jesus said, "Father, forgive them, for they do not know what they are doing."*
> (Luke 23:34)

The early Church called Stephen, a man full of faith and the Holy Spirit, to serve as a deacon.[7] One day, a group of religious men picked an argument with him but couldn't stand up to Stephen's wisdom, knowledge, and spirit. Their rebellious hearts hardened as they heard the Holy Spirit speak truths of the Scriptures through Stephen, and they dragged him out of the city to stone him to death.

---

6. Matthew 5:21–23.
7. Acts 6:5.

Stephen stood strong. Even when he was one stone away from death, he held to his Christlike attitude. He looked up into heaven with a prayerful plea that God would not hold this sin against them. He held onto the heart and mind of Christ even as the people threw the last stone to silence him. May this be the attitude of our hearts.

> *Then he fell on his knees and cried out, "Lord, do not hold this sin against them."*
> (Acts 7:60)

Every person who has ever confessed faith in Jesus Christ has a cross to bear, a weakness to overcome. Our weak point may be the result of harm done to us or a genetic fluke of nature. As an example: when a child grows up with addicts or alcoholics for parents, they live in an atmosphere of lies and deceit. Because of this, they must constantly fight against an inherited proclivity for lying and deception. If a child grows up in a family where money, property, and material things are coveted symbols of success and status, they have to overcome these attitudes and see them crucified with Christ.

We cannot serve two masters. Delicious red apples and sour crabapples never grow naturally on the same tree. In the same way, lies, deceit, and covetousness will not grow on the same branches that bear the fruit of the Spirit. Lawless attitudes and pursuits cannot blossom and grow on the same limb as the sweet fruit of the Holy Spirit.

What tree will you be grafted onto?

> *But the fruit of the Spirit is love, joy, peace, forbearance, kindness, goodness, faithfulness, gentleness and self-control. Against such things there is no law.*
> *Those who belong to Christ Jesus have crucified the flesh with its passions and desires.*
> (Galatians 5:22–24)

There are sure consequences for those who make themselves an enemy to everyone around them. Their thieving, violent ways are despicable to all but their like-minded villainous friends. This lifestyle brings a lawless person to ruin. They will end up with a life that is like sand slipping through their fingers.

And there they lay on the sidewalk for us to trip over. They broke into our home, stole our valuables, and pawned them so they could get a few bucks. Now they are broken, hungry, and thirsty, spread out in front of our morning coffee shop.

Right there in front of us lies a neighbor, and because of this we buy her a bagel and a bottle of water. Then, the Spirit prompts us to offer the help they desperately need. If their hearts change, we will all be the better for it. If not, our help will cause their conscience to see their depravity and its consequences.

If your enemy is hungry, feed him; if he is thirsty, give him something to drink. In doing this, you will heap burning coals on his head.
(Romans 12:20)

When God told Jonah to go to Nineveh to call the people of this great city to repent, he marched to the nearest port and bought a ticket on the first ship sailing the opposite direction. He had a good reason. The Ninevites were a violent, dreadful people. Jonah didn't want the enemies of Israel to have a chance to repent and receive forgiveness and mercy. He knew they deserved the harshest of all judgments because they were a lawless people. But God's purpose prevailed. Jonah ended up in Nineveh after the whale that swallowed him belched him up on the beach. The people of Nineveh heard his message and repented. God forgave them and showed them mercy.

Now, in the age of the church, a once lawless people who never sought after God have the law of love written on their hearts. This is the law of freedom, not of external legal limits on what we do or say, but an internal law etched on the very depths of our being. This is the law of love that causes our hearts to show mercy to undeserving souls. This New Covenant law of love compels us to go to those who are unworthy and share the Good News that gives life. We go with our feet secured in Gospel shoes to call people to repentance, then proclaim forgiveness and mercy. All those who deserve God's just and righteous judgments are beckoned to repent, call on the name of the Lord, and receive Jesus as Savior.

Will you go speak to your neighbor?

Will you be a messenger of forgiveness and mercy?

Speak and act as those who are going to be judged by the law that gives freedom, because judgment without mercy will be shown to anyone who has not been merciful. Mercy triumphs over judgment.
(James 2:12–13)

At first blush, the previous verse sounds moralistic. It may come across as an external law to restrain natural inclinations. A better way is when our efforts to help friends, family, and neighbors flow from the heart where the law of love is written and flourishing. It's possible to forgive an offense when the Prince of Peace reigns in our hearts. Words that hurt us can be pardoned because we have the mind of Christ. Indeed, our love serves to cover people who once harmed us by their words and deeds.

The Old Testament Law said: an eye for an eye, wrong for wrong, or tit for tat. Our Lord Jesus has fulfilled the law by taking that payback upon Himself. The revenge we planned against our enemy got nailed to the cross. Our right to get revenge died with Jesus on Mount Calvary.

> *Make sure that nobody pays back wrong for wrong,*
> *but always strive to do what is good for each other and for everyone else.*
> (1 Thessalonians 5:15)

When we expect someone to tolerate an enemy, we ask a lot. In reality, the call to love our enemies is downright impossible. Our natural inclination is to hope our enemy will suffer for what they did to us. That guy who cut us off stirred up a rage inside of us and we want to laugh when they get pulled over and ticketed. But that is contrary to the law of love written on our hearts.

What is written on our hearts keeps us from taking vengeance. It stops us when we want to mock our enemy when he gets his just deserts. This law of love implanted in us compels us to go the extra mile. What is indelibly written in our heart of hearts makes it possible to forgive readily and to offer mercy for even the bitterest offense against us. Instead of the bitter fruit of revenge, we will produce the sweet fruits of the spirit—love, joy, and peace.

To forgive an enemy is an act of love that frees us from being bound up in bitterness and anger. This forgiveness is only possible because the Spirit of Christ has written the law of love on our hearts.

10. Love Your Enemies
Q & A

1. What is the difference between Old Testament Law written in stone and the law of love written on our hearts?

2. How can we deal with our anger toward those who have hurt or offended us?

3. How did Jesus show love toward His enemies as He hung on the cross?

4. What is the effect of the law of love that is written on our hearts?

My Journal Notes:

Chapter 11
Love's Promise

Key Scriptures:

- "For I command you today to love the LORD your God, to walk in obedience to him, and to keep his commands, decrees and laws; then you will live and increase, and the LORD your God will bless you in the land you are entering to possess." (Deuteronomy 30:16)

- "This day I call the heavens and the earth as witnesses against you that I have set before you life and death, blessings and curses. Now choose life, so that you and your children may live and that you may love the LORD your God, listen to his voice, and hold fast to him. For the LORD is your life, and he will give you many years in the land he swore to give to your fathers, Abraham, Isaac and Jacob." (Deuteronomy 30:19–20)

In this study, we'll come to know the promises of God's love that are as sure as forever; from the beginning with no end. This topic instructs us so we can be certain of our bond of fellowship and its many benefits. We will find assurance in the multiple aspects of our heavenly Father's love-inspired words that welcome us into the safety of His dwelling place.

This is not an "if you're a good boy I'll give you a cookie" kind of promise. God's covenant is pure and everlasting. His love-inspired promises are as solid as New Jerusalem's foundations of precious stones: jasper, sapphire, chalcedony, emeralds, sardonyx, carnelian, chrysolite, beryl, topaz, chrysoprase, jacinth, and amethyst. His assurances are as strong as the city's walls of jasper. God's oaths are as enduring and beautiful as each of the heavenly city's gates made of a single pearl.[1]

Loving Christ is not a "tit for tat" kind of affection, nor is it a "yin and yang" kind of relationship. It is not reciprocal altruism. In fact, the Lord Almighty is God who brings us into covenant with Him, and He is faithful to keep our covenant relationship strong. The Lord is our strength to endure to the end. In Christ Jesus we are made overcomers, and He is faithful to the end, even when we are not.[2]

We enter into covenant with our heavenly Father when we are made new creations in Christ, and His promise is sure—never ending. There is great peace in this assurance. We can trust in His promises. We can set our anchor in God's word because Christ is the Rock in whom we anchor.

1. Revelation 21:18–21.
2. 2 Timothy 2:13.

Entering into God's covenant promise is like being brought into a land of plenty. And yet, the New Covenant is not a specific geographic location. Instead, our place of promise is in Christ and His eternal kingdom. We can't use a road map to find the way, saying it is in this city or town, or over there on that far away mountain, because God's kingdom is in us, ever near us, and encompassing us. A map of planets and stars will never show us the way to God's promised eternal kingdom.

When we come into covenant with Christ, it's not as if He comes to bust open a piñata of blessings over our head. It's not like an Easter egg hunt to find blessings to fill our baskets like candy. Instead, when we become disciples of our Lord Jesus, we step under heaven's aegis. Picture it as being covered by Jesus' prayer shawl where His prayers of blessing are answered on our behalf. The blessed promises of the kingdom of heaven become ours as we take refuge under the wings of Jesus' garment of righteousness that He spreads over us.

When we are brought into the realm of the kingdom, we come into God's promised and sure protection. We can bask in His abundant provision and healing presence. The Scriptures give us many word pictures to delight in and help us understand our covenant that protects us with His love.

> *Turn your ear to me, come quickly to my rescue;*
> *be my rock of refuge, a strong fortress to save me.*
> (Psalm 31:2)

When Jesus prayed His High Priestly prayer for His present and future disciples, He offered a prayer for all time. That prayer, prayed over two-thousand years ago, still covers us because His words are not limited by time or space. Jesus' prayer garment had a hem and four corners with tzitzit, or cords of blue tassels.[3] The woman who came to Jesus because she suffered with an "issue of blood" touched the tzitzit of Jesus' prayer shawl, knowing that she would be healed.[4] The power and effect of Jesus' prayers still cover His followers from that day until the end of time.

Our prayers are powerful and effective when we pray as if touching the threads, the cords, the tassels, and the very fabric of Jesus' prayers. When we call on the Lord in agreement with Jesus' High Priestly prayer, we strengthen the fabric of the kingdom of heaven. As we intercede the way Jesus taught us, our petitions will be in keeping with all righteousness. The effective and fervent prayers of godly people will be in agreement with all Jesus' pleas and promises.[5] As we echo Jesus' prayers our voices cry out in a perfect harmonious love song.

---

3. Deuteronomy 22:12.
4. Luke 8:43–48.
5. James 5:16.

> *He will cover you with his feathers, and under his wings you will find refuge;*
> *his faithfulness will be your shield and rampart.*
> (Psalm 91:4)

Our Lord God and Father is ever-present with us, especially in times of trouble. This is a sure and lasting promise. We can stand bold and strong in the face of trouble, because we hold onto the promise of His saving grace. When we go into battle in life's jungle, the Lord sends us out protected with His armor. The Lord Almighty gives us His battle gear as a confirmation of His covenant of love.

When we are fully armored, we brandish the sword of the Spirit, which is the word of God. A shield of faith protects us from the fiery arrows of the enemy. The hope of our salvation serves as a helmet of protection for our head. His breastplate is righteousness to guard our hearts. Truth is fastened around us like a belt to gird us and bind us to the Lord who is God of the armies of heaven. The truth of the Gospel prepares our feet to go out into battle. We press forward to take the light of the Good News to push back against the darkness of this world. Our whole purpose as we go into battle is to win the peace. Indeed, we battle side by side with the Prince of Peace. Then, the Gospel message brings salvation by faith, and gives lost souls peace with our heavenly Father and Christ Jesus, our Prince of Peace.

> *Contend, LORD, with those who contend with me;*
> *fight against those who fight against me.*
> *Take up shield and armor; arise and come to my aid.*
> *Brandish spear and javelin against those who pursue me.*
> *Say to me, "I am your salvation."*
> (Psalm 35:1–3)

The best place to pitch our tent is in an encampment surrounded by heavenly hosts. In this campsite, there is no need to fear the horrors of the night, nor the arrows that fly by day.[6] The firebrands of the enemy will not harm us. The pandemics that lurk in the dark cannot destroy us, nor can they afflict or crush us at high noon. When we walk in reverence, awe, and in delighted obedience before the Lord, we need not fear any one because we are encircled by heaven's angelic protectors.

> *The angel of the LORD encamps around those who fear him,*
> *and he delivers them.*
> (Psalm 34:7)

---

6. Psalm 91:5.

Like palm trees that surround a desert oasis, the Lord shelters us from the burning heat of this dry and parched land.[7] The shifting sands of the desert may burn our feet, but the spring water cools and refreshes us. The Lord shelters us in the cleft of the rock from so the raging storms will not sweep us away. God is our covering, our canopy, our hiding place, and an ever-present help in the day of trouble. The Lord God is present with us through life's journey like a mother who lovingly covers her sleeping child for the night and then greets her with a sweet morning song. Like a cloud by day and a pillar of fire by night He shelters us.

> *It will be a shelter and shade from the heat of the day,*
> *and a refuge and hiding place from the storm and rain.*
> (Isaiah 4:6)

The Bible provides beautiful word pictures of Jesus, our Good Shepherd who lovingly cares for the sheep of His pasture. In the morning, He calls each one in the sheepfold by name. The fold's Gatekeeper is the Spirit of Christ who opens the gate for the sheep to be led into fresh, green pasture. The Good Shepherd doesn't drive the flock to pasture, but goes ahead of them to clear the way of any danger and to lead them. When little lambs get weak and stumble, He gathers them in His arms and holds them close to His heart.[8]

The sheep follow Him because they know His voice, and it's a comfort to hear their names called out should they begin to wander from the safety of the flock. At every moment of the day or night we, like sheep, are encompassed in the Good Shepherd's loving, protective care. We know His voice and follow as He leads us into God's eternal rest.

> *The gatekeeper opens the gate for him, and the sheep listen to his voice.*
> *He calls his own sheep by name and leads them out.*
> *When he has brought out all his own, he goes on ahead of them,*
> *and his sheep follow him because they know his voice.*
> (John 10:3–4)

Troubled times bring never ending pandemics, earthquakes, wildfires, tsunamis, hurricanes, and tornadoes. And yet, all those who come to Christ find refuge because Jesus' petitions shelter us like a prayer shawl. We are covered by the wings of His intercessions on our behalf. The Gospel of John gives us a record of Jesus' High Priestly prayer for all of His present and future followers. He prayed and His followers were covered in the shadow of His wings. His powerful prayer continues to cover us and is a refuge to us in these perilous times.

---

7. Psalm 63:1.
8. Isaiah 40:11.

This is the invaluable, all-encompassing nature of God's love for all of creation. Those who trust in God's unfailing love are surrounded with a hedge of protection, a mighty fortress, a shield, the Rock of refuge, the strongholds of the kingdom of heaven, and the assurance of God's power and might to save.[9]

> *How priceless is your unfailing love, O God!*
> *People take refuge in the shadow of your wings.*
> (Psalm 36:7)

As Jesus pressed on toward Jerusalem, He lamented over the city where the prophets were killed and God's messengers stoned. Later, as Jesus made His triumphal entry into the city, He wept because the people were spiritually blind and would not recognize the Messiah in His time. But all those whose eyes are opened and confess Jesus as the Christ are covered with His feathers as a hen covers her chicks.

Jesus wept because His heart desired to gather God's people and protect them. The crowds shouted "Hosannah!" as Jesus rode triumphant into the city on a donkey's colt. But just a few days later, the same crowd would shout, "Crucify, Crucify!"

> *How often I have longed to gather your children together,*
> *as a hen gathers her chicks under her wings.*
> (Luke 13:34)

The Lord Almighty's dwelling is a welcoming place, a delightful abode, and a safe sanctuary. Those who enter this shelter find favor and a place of quiet refuge.[10] This is a special habitation because its doors swing wide open to welcome the fatherless, widows, orphans, the weak, and those held captive to sin. Indeed, all those who are alone and in need of protection[11] find a refuge here.

In this holy place, love's promise is fulfilled. The congregation gathers at His footstool to worship, serve, and minister in harmony with Christ Jesus, our High Priest. This is a place of rest where we are seated with our Lord Jesus[12] who ushers us into God's holy presence covered with His robe of righteousness. God's holy sanctuary is a place where joyful songs burst out like the morning lily opening its blossom to the sun.

---

9. Psalm 18:2.
10. Psalm 84:1, Exodus 15:17.
11. Psalm 68:5.
12. Ephesians 2:6.

> *Let us go to his dwelling place, let us worship at his footstool, saying,*
> *"Arise, Lord, and come to your resting place, you and the ark of your might.*
> *May your priests be clothed with your righteousness;*
> *may your faithful people sing for joy."*
> (Psalm 132:7–9)

Those who are called into covenant with Christ become like a holy mountain that cannot be shaken. God's covenant children are encircled by mountains of protection. They are surrounded both now and forever. The seven mountains surrounding Jerusalem stand like high towers of defense to protect the city. The people of Israel trekked up the dusty, dangerous mountain roads, singing their songs of ascent, to go and worship at the temple in Jerusalem. But we have a better covenant. We ascend to worship on Mount Zion, the city of the living God, and the heavenly Jerusalem where Jesus serves as High Priest. In this place, we come together with thousands of holy angels to join in joyful assembly to worship the Creator of all heaven and earth.

Everyone whose name is written in the Book of Life may join this holy assembly. In this holy place of worship, we are sprinkled with the blood of the new covenant that speaks to God on behalf of sinners. The power of Jesus' blood is greater than Abel's blood that cried out for vengeance, because the blood of Christ pleads for mercy.[13] This is an unshakeable truth where we anchor our souls.

> *Those who trust in the Lord are like Mount Zion,*
> *which cannot be shaken but endures forever.*
> *As the mountains surround Jerusalem,*
> *so the Lord surrounds his people both now and forevermore.*
> (Psalm 125:1–2)

A wall of protective fire encompasses us and drives away those who would prey upon God's covenant people. Gideon showed us a great example of this as he rescued His people from the nation's oppressors. Then he served victorious as Israel's judge. The battle tactics the Lord instructed him to use offer us a beautiful picture of the Lord of the Armies of Heaven who promises to surround us with a wall of fire. Gideon sent all but 100 men home from the battle. Each of the remaining men were given a pot with a torch inside and a trumpet. He divided the army into three groups, who then surrounded the Midianite army. At Gideon's signal, they broke their pots, blew their horns, held up the flaming torches, and shouted, "A sword for the Lord and for Gideon!" Then, they stood still while the fighting men in the enemies' army turned on each other and ran away in fear.

---
13. Hebrews 12:20–24.

> *"And I myself will be a wall of fire around it," declares the LORD,*
> *"and I will be its glory within."*
> (Zechariah 2:5)

The Father's dwelling is a place of wonders and He has given us an estate within this pleasant garden. Our bond of covenant opens the gate into this lovely dwelling place, a planting of the Lord.[14] Those who remain in His dwelling find refuge and safety. All who keep the covenant will dwell in His presence, covered as a chick is covered by a hen's protective feathers. As long as we abide in His presence, partake of His manifest presence, and dwell in His holy dwelling, we can enjoy rest and pleasant pastures.

Safety and security in the Father's dwelling place are the promise and fulfillment of God's loving kindness toward us.

> *How lovely is your dwelling place, LORD Almighty!*
> (Psalm 84:1)

This powerful love binds us together with the Father, the Son, and Holy Spirit. This same love is the glue that has held the church together through centuries of tests, trials, and turbulence. Love's promise prevents the gates of hell from prevailing in their war against the church.[15] God's loving kindness strengthens the bond of fellowship that keeps God's people united as one with Christ. Love calls us to wisdom, and wisdom builds a strong house with seven pillars. In this house, wisdom prepares a banquet table before us.[16]

In the embrace of God's abundant, all-encompassing love, we come into the blessings of bountiful provision and the security of God's favor. Awash in heaven's love, we find freedom from the chains that once bound us. The grip of those who oppress us and deal with us violently is broken and we are set free in Christ Jesus our Lord and Savior.

> *The trees will yield their fruit and the ground will yield its crops;*
> *the people will be secure in their land. They will know that I am the LORD,*
> *when I break the bars of their yoke*
> *and rescue them from the hands of those who enslaved them.*
> (Ezekiel 34:27)

---

14. Isaiah 61:3.
15. Matthew 16:18.
16. Proverbs 9:1–6.

11. Love's Promise
Q & A

1. Describe the covenantal bond of love between the Father and all those who are called by His holy name.

2. How do we enter into Love's promise?

3. Does Jesus' High Priestly prayer, prayed almost 2000 years ago, still cover us today?

4. Where will you pitch your tent?

5. Where will you anchor your soul?

My Journal Notes:

Chapter 12
Enduring Love

Key Scriptures:

- "Through Jesus, therefore, let us continually offer to God a sacrifice of praise—the fruit of lips that openly profess his name." (Hebrews 13:15)
- "He who made the Pleiades and Orion, who turns midnight into dawn and darkens day into night, who calls for the waters of the sea and pours them out over the face of the land—the LORD is his name." (Amos 5:8)

The Psalmist begins Psalm 136 with an inspired proclamation of his good purpose: "Give thanks to the Lord." Then, he tells us the reason for his thanksgiving: "for he is good." This study brings to light the beautiful words of praise that flow through this song. This love psalm overflows with affections and pours out expressions of gratitude. All because the Lord is good and has shown His love toward His people. From the writer's words, we learn that the Creator's love emanates from His very nature. Every blessing poured out upon His people, and every vengeance unleashed on His enemies on behalf of His people, are all acts of love. The Father's love conquers all.

This study is a verse by verse meditation on the many aspects of God's abundant love toward the sheep of His pasture. Every bold statement the Psalmist sings out inspires the congregation's jubilant response: *"His love endures forever."* With each proclamation and joyful reply, we come to a greater understanding of God's all-encompassing love. It's as if the Psalmist wrote the verses of his song of thanksgiving so that we may sing with them, adding verse upon verse to offer up our thanksgiving in the congregation, inspired by God's overwhelming love.

"Give thanks to the LORD, for he is good."

The very elements of God's nature radiate with goodness, righteousness, justice, mercy, loving kindness, and enduring love. Every word of creation, act of justice, show of mercy, and hand of provision are evidences of His love toward all humankind.

"His love endures forever."

"Give thanks to the God of gods."

There are no other gods who can compare with Elohim. Indeed, all others who set themselves up as gods are princes of darkness.[1] These false gods are fallen angels, created imaginings, or made by the hands of men. They have eyes but cannot see, ears but cannot hear. They have mouths but cannot speak. Counterfeit gods have no hearts, only wood, stone, and idolatrous flesh. But the God we serve sees everything. He hears every cry and groan when we suffer. The Father's loving heart is like that of a dad who holds his newborn child, counts his fingers, toes, and even the hair on his head. The Lord Almighty hears every word spoken throughout all the Earth, and in every moment of time. By the power of His word and the power of His Holy Spirit, the Lord God speaks to whom He will speak by means of the holy Scriptures, the whisper of the Holy Spirit, dreams, and prophetic oracles. Our God is above all.

"His love endures forever."

"Give thanks to the Lord of lords."

Every leader, whether king, queen, president, governor, mayor, or tribal chief, serves under the hand of Adonai who is Sovereign over all who rule on Earth. The Lord Almighty raises up and deposes leaders according to His purpose and plan. God establishes and throws down nations because of His enduring love for those who are called by His holy name.

"His love endures forever."

"To him who alone does great wonders."

The Word of creation spoke into the Earth's chaotic void to fill it with wonders. Since then, every child conceived and born upon the Earth is another of the Creator's great wonders. The seed buried in the fertile soil and watered by rainfall springs forth with life and grows to be a mighty oak tree in the forest, revealing another wonder of creation. A greater wonder is saving a lost soul. The redemptive blood of the Lamb of God is the greatest manifestation of the Father's love-driven wonders.

"His love endures forever."

---

1. Ephesians 6:12, Colossians 1:16, 2:15.

"Who by his understanding made the heavens."

By the Word of Wisdom, God stretched out the universe, and by the Word all things are held together.[2] The sun, moon and stars manifest the Creator's love, wisdom, and power. They will remain as His faithful witnesses in the skies until the end of time.

"His love endures forever."

"Who spread out the earth upon the waters."

By the Word and out of water all things were created.[3] The Creator raised up islands, peninsulas, and continents out of the chaotic darkness that stewed over the surface of the deep.[4] Upon the continents, He formed mountain peaks to gather the snow. The Almighty God shaped the hills, plateaus, and plains where the rains would fall to make them flourish to feed humankind and all the wild animals. And He placed this beautiful earth in the care of Adam and Eve and all who would follow in their footsteps.

"His love endures forever."

"Who made the great lights—"

On the first day of creation, the Word spoke, saying, "Let there be light." The light's great purpose is to drive back the darkness "over the surface of the deep." In that moment, light and darkness were separated, each for God's good purpose. The stars were set in place—in precise proximity to each other. The great lights rotate in their orbits in an orderly manner throughout the vast, immeasurable universe. Indeed, who can bind the chains of the Pleiades? Who can loosen Orion's belt?[5]

"His love endures forever."

"The sun to govern the day."

The sun's light shines out upon the earth to serve humankind. It blazes out to color the sky with hues of red and gold, announcing the morning. The sun rises above us to warm the earth, make it grow and flourish, and then settles behind the mountains with a blaze of glory. The dawn's painted sky warns of storms to come. The evening blushes with shades of red as a promise of good weather to make our gardens grow.

"His love endures forever."

---

2. Colossians 1:17.
3. 2 Peter 3:5.
4. Genesis 1:2.
5. Job 38:31

"The moon and stars to govern the night."

The light of the moon shines for those who trek along shadowy pathways through the night. Lovers linger close and wax poetic in the light of a full moon. The new moon and full moon pass above us in elliptical orbits. A blood moon engulfs us with wonder and the hunter's moon fills the woodsman with anticipation. The Earth's lone orb alters its course as it goes from crescent to full, from a sliver of light to a full harvest moon.

The luminaries in the sky are beacons that give direction to the nomad and voyager as they go on their way through the night. The voices of the stars sing out to proclaim the glories of the Creator.

"His love endures forever."

"To him who struck down the firstborn of Egypt."

The Psalmist takes a turn here to show us another aspect of God's unfailing love: His justice. Yahweh heard the groans of His enslaved people and, because of His faithfulness and righteousness, He rose up against the enemies of Israel. Indeed, without acts of justice against oppressors who harm His people, God's love would be an empty promise. With the tenth and final plague against Egypt, Yahweh's angel of judgment struck down all the firstborn sons who were not covered by the blood of a lamb on the doorposts of their homes. This served as the final conquering blow of God's love-driven justice against the Egyptian oppressors.

"His love endures forever."

"And brought Israel out from among them."

The angel of judgment's final assault against Egypt accomplished the Lord's good purpose. Finally, Pharaoh's hardened heart turned away from oppression and rebellion and he set God's people free. The death of his eldest son broke the heart of this unbending ruler.

"His love endures forever."

"With a mighty hand and outstretched arm."

God Almighty's hand of judgment stretched over the oppressors in Egypt and at the same time He stretched a protective hand over His people in the Land of Goshen. Yahweh placed a rod in Moses' hand to wreak judgment and redemption. It served as a weapon of war against oppressors and a shepherd's rod to comfort the people.

"His love endures forever."

"To him who divided the Red Sea asunder."

Moses held God's scepter of authority in his hand. The armies of Egypt pressed in on the encampment of Israel and trapped them against the shores of the Red Sea. The people shouted out their complaints against Moses. They confronted him with their angry fears. They shouted at Moses, "Was it because there were no graves in Egypt that you brought us to the desert to die?"[6] Then the Lord asked Moses the question of the moment: "Why are you crying out to me? Tell the Israelites to move on." Even in their moment of fear, and in spite of their complaints, God made a way—an impossible way—for His people to escape from an army of chariots led by Pharaoh whose heart had become hardened once again. Moses held out the rod over the Red Sea and the sea divided with walls of water on either side of a dry pathway for them to cross over.

"His love endures forever."

"And brought Israel through the midst of it."

This miraculous deliverance freed an enslaved people. They were repressed, beaten, and pushed beyond the limit of human endurance by inhuman oppressors. Jehovah God heard their cry and made a way for the deliverance of His people.

"His love endures forever."

"But swept Pharaoh and his army into the Red Sea."

Egypt's army and armed chariots charged headlong into the pathway through the sea. By a miracle of Yahweh's justice, Israel's pursuers were crushed as the walls of water crashed in on them. God's people gathered together, safe on the other side of the sea, and they sang out with joy because the horses and riders who would have overwhelmed them were crushed in the tidal flood.

"His love endures forever."

"To him who led his people through the wilderness."

A cloud covered God's people by day and a pillar of fire shielded them through the night. The cloud and pillar of fire would lead the people through the desert. The Great I AM led them into a wasteland with no water. The sparse grasslands were not enough for their flocks, and the land produced no crops for a wandering people to gather. But God who Provides surrounded them and covered them in a dry and thirsty land.

"His love endures forever."

---

6. Exodus 14:11.

"To him who struck down great kings."

Kings ruled their domains in the wilderness that God's people passed through. They were seated on thrones of their own glory to reign over their people. They gathered mighty armies to fight and annihilate the tribes of Israel. But Moses spoke powerful words to greet each morning: "Arise, O Lord, may your enemies be scattered." Jehovah God did arise and He overthrew the enemies who would have destroyed His people.

"His love endures forever."

"And killed mighty kings–"

The mightiest of Earth's kings cannot stand against the King of kings. The Lord Almighty places rulers on their thrones and He also deposes them. They rose up with evil intentions toward the people God delivered from captivity. For the honor of His holy name, God threw down these grand and legendary monarchs.

"His love endures forever."

"Sihon king of the Amorites."

The wandering tribes of Israel were still east of the Jordan River when they asked the king's permission to cross through his land in peace. They even offered to pay for the water they would use. But King Sihon would have none of it. Instead, he gathered his subjects together and drew up battle lines against Israel. He and his people were struck down and Israel took possession of their land.

"His love endures forever."

"And Og king of Bashan–"

The king who reigned over the land of Bashan rallied his troops and sent an army to rout God's people. But this king raised his weapons against a holy people to his own demise. God's protective love for his people required that Og be overthrown.

"His love endures forever."

"And gave their land as an inheritance."

In victory, Moses allocated King Sihon's conquered lands to the tribe of Manasseh. This vast territory became known as a land of plenty where the cattle grew fat. Their portion of the land of milk and honey would produce many abundant harvests.

"His love endures forever."

"An inheritance to his servant Israel."

Joseph was sold as a slave and he suffered in the land that enslaved him. His master threw him in prison for an offense he didn't commit. And yet, years later, he forgave and restored his brothers in their time of need. He set a feast from his own table before them.[7] After he died, the tribes of Israel carried his bones back to the land of promise and his son's descendants were allotted the land of the kings who fought to destroy them. The good Lord brought them out of bondage and set the boundaries of their inheritance in pleasant places.[8]

"His love endures forever."

"He remembered us in our low estate."

God's people were delivered from slavery in a foreign land. They had been downtrodden and beaten. The burden on their shoulders was too heavy and the gathering baskets in their hands an overwhelming burden. God heard their cry that rose up from the land of their servitude. God acted in mercy. Indeed, the richness of His glory and the power of His might were made manifest in weak vessels.

"His love endures forever."

"And freed us from our enemies."

By mighty acts and outstretched arm, the Great I AM delivered His people from the land that enslaved them. Their trials provide us with a living illustration of God's power and might to save us from the clutches of darkness, the evil grip of sin's consequences, and the enslaving power of sin.

"His love endures forever."

"He gives food to every creature."

In the land of Bashan, herds grazed in lush, well-watered pastures. God's people thrived as they lived off the fat of the land. The fields of grain produced thirty, sixty, or a hundred-fold of the seed sown. The oxen, donkeys, cattle, goats, and sheep could rest under the shade trees to chew their cud, fully satisfied.

"His love endures forever."

---

7. Genesis 43:33–34.
8. Psalm 16:6.

"Give thanks to the God of heaven."

Grateful hearts compel us to lift up holy hands in thanksgiving because the God who delivered Israel from the bondage of slavery has not changed. His mercies endure forever. He raised up Christ Jesus, our Messiah who gave Himself as a blood sacrifice so that we may be redeemed by His atoning blood. We are set free from enslavement to sin's darkness. We have a great promise of eternal blessings where there will be no more sorrow, no more tears.

"His love endures forever."

The Psalm begins and ends with prayerful thanksgiving. God is worthy of all praise because of the boundless, love-saturated light He established on the first day of creation. The Creator's Spirit hovered over the chaotic waters that encompassed the earth. What the Creator began in love continues to thrive in love and flourish in the light of righteousness. Now, in Christ, we have a great promise of an eternity where love rules supreme in a city that does not need the sun or moon to shine on it, for the Glory of God gives it light, and the Lamb is its lamp.[9]

This is a love that reaches far, stretches out wide, dives deep, shoots high, is poured out in abundance, and is as vast as the universe. Our Lord Jesus holds this love out to us in His nail-scarred hands. Every facet of His love is awesome to behold. Every aspect of His love is beyond our capacity to comprehend because this is an ever-enduring and triumphant love offered to all of humankind who will receive.

> *I pray that out of his glorious riches he may strengthen you with power through his Spirit in your inner being, so that Christ may dwell in your hearts through faith. And I pray that you, being rooted and established in love, may have power, together with all the Lord's holy people, to grasp how wide and long and high and deep is the love of Christ.*
> (Ephesians 3:16–18)

---

9. Revelation 21:23.

12. Enduring Love
Q & A

1. What is your heart's response to the Psalmist's proclamations of God's love?

2. Who can compare with the Lord God who created all the heavens and earth?

3. What is the greatest of all God's wonders?

4. Explain how justice makes God's love complete.

My Journal Notes:

Chapter 13
Loving Discipline

Key Scriptures:

- "My son, do not despise the Lords' discipline, and do not resent his rebuke, because the Lord disciplines those he loves, as a father the son he delights in." (Proverbs 3:11–12)

- "And have you completely forgotten this word of encouragement that addresses you as a father addresses his son? It says, 'My son, do not make light of the Lord's discipline, and do not lose heart when he rebukes you, because the Lord disciplines the one he loves, and he chastens everyone he accepts as his son.' Endure hardship as discipline; God is treating you as his children. For what children are not disciplined by their father? If you are not disciplined—and everyone undergoes discipline—then you are not legitimate, not true sons and daughters at all. Moreover, we have all had human fathers who disciplined us and we respected them for it. How much more should we submit to the Father of spirits and live! They disciplined us for a little while as they thought best; but God disciplines us for our good, in order that we may share in his holiness. No discipline seems pleasant at the time, but painful. Later on, however, it produces a harvest of righteousness and peace for those who have been trained by it." (Hebrews 12:5–11)

There are times in our Christian life that this narrow path seems to have a prickly cactus boundary. When we slip up, we get scratched and poked until we get back on track to live in accord with God's precepts. Because the Father loves us so much, His desire is to keep us in close fellowship and He disciplines His children to bring us back to walk as Jesus walked—in the shelter of His presence.

In this study, we'll come to understand God's love-driven discipline toward His sons and daughters who are called by His holy name. We'll learn about the hard work that love requires, and why it's often a job that we would rather ignore or leave to someone else. The guiding principles Jesus taught with regard to discipline are the focus of this study. This study takes a look at the application of discipline in the church and why it's such a thorny issue. We'll learn about the loving discipline that's a necessary part of Christian gatherings.

Parents have a strong, natural protective love for their children. When we're out on a walk with little Johnny and he starts to wander off the sidewalk to and explore in a ditch filled with briars, critters, and snakes, we will bring him to our side to protect him. A good parent will call him back so he can walk with Dad and be safe.

You know how a dad responds when his son wanders.

"Hey, get back here, Johnny." A parent's words are clear and emphatic. If the son ignores Dad, the words become clearer and forceful:

"John Marshall Timson, get back here right now!"

If Johnny persists in wandering, Dad's nurturing hand will bring him back. But when his son breaks the rules and sneaks out of the yard to explore on his own, he will learn the lesson the hard way after he falls into a patch of cactus needles as he tries to catch that lizard.

Our heavenly Father is very patient with us. He first speaks to us through His word, the Bible, to warn us about the hazards of wandering away from the safety of His presence and from the safeguards of our covenant in Christ. When we dismiss the written word, our Father may send a friend to offer a tactful word of correction. If our ears are closed to this warning, our itchy feet will get us caught like a sheep tangled in briars. There are times when the Good Shepherd allows us to experience the natural consequences of our sins, and yet He is always ready to hear our repentant cry. If we persist in wandering, He may impose consequences that will bring us back. When we call out to Him from the entanglements of our sin, He will come with His shepherd staff to rescue us—all because of His abundant love.

Even though I walk through the darkest valley, I will fear no evil, for you are with me; your rod and your staff, they comfort me.
(Psalm 23:4)

The Father's discipline is personal and always clear to us. But when this step of correction is rejected, our sin must be dealt with in the Christian community. For this reason, Jesus gives us parameters for exercising discipline in our gatherings. The title given for His teaching in many Bibles is: "Dealing With Sin in the Church." This lesson is central to cohesive Christian fellowship and worship.

It's important to understand that the Creator established the foundation of all truth in the beginning.[1] In seven days of creation, God brought order out of chaos, and He still asserts order wherever His holy name is proclaimed.

---

1. The author's book *Great Separations* teaches on this topic.

It may well be said: "Where two or three are gathered together there will be offenses." These failures are caused by self-serving sins. Disorder is the result of living in a fallen world, caused by rebellion against truth and righteousness. If the offense is not dealt with, it will fester like gangrene and bring the whole fellowship to ruin. Wise, gentle, and godly discipline restores order.

One great weakness in the American Church is that many of its members refuse discipline. Submission to authority isn't our cup of tea. It's impossible to confront issues when one sour note causes a family to stomp out the door and never return. Another challenge is when Christian leaders impose judgments, but forget generous applications of forgiveness and mercy. A lack of discipline and harsh, unmerciful authority are two extremes that will tear a fellowship apart. Jesus' instructions in Matthew Chapter 18 show us a better way. The paths of admonishment and correction are replete with pitfalls, but we can't ignore this part of Christian life. These hazards can be managed as we follow the pathway charted for us in Jesus' teaching, because it is centered in love.

Let's take Jesus' instructions on church discipline one step at a time. Each point makes it clear that this process, while difficult, serves to bring godly order to our gatherings. As we consider these steps, remember that this discipline is only for those who are in Christ and not applicable to those who are not part of a Christian community.

The first step Jesus prescribes is to go directly to the person who committed the offense. Don't wait for them to come to you. This is a one-on-one talk about what they did and how you felt harmed by it. If we talk about the problem to people who are not involved, it causes more harm than good. But don't hesitate to ask for counsel from a friend who will keep your confidence. Avoid broadcasting prayer requests, because it can quickly turn into nothing but pious-sounding gossip. Spreading rumors may be worse than the original offense and could undermine the whole process.

Ask the offender to sit down over coffee or tea where no one else can hear you. Talk it through with them. When hearts are right and correction is spoken with love and mercy, this will bring about the very best outcome. Forgiveness will cleanse away the offense and restore Christians to sweet fellowship in Christ.

To be clear, confronting someone in person isn't always possible and may not be safe. If the offender is an abusive, violent, or predatory person, you don't want to put yourself in a place where you're vulnerable to verbal abuse or physical attack. There may also be the danger of getting caught up in their smooth talk and acceding to their temptations.[2] If the offender is of the op-

---
2. Galatians 6:1.

posite gender, it's a good idea to take someone with you. When there is a risk of physical danger, you should be sure to ask a trusted leader to go with you or go in your stead to the one-on-one meeting.

Either way, when your offender listens and regrets what they have done, you have an opportunity to forgive, restore, and strengthen the relationship. The bond of friendship will be stronger than ever and healthy boundaries will be established.

> *If your brother or sister sins, go and point out their fault, just between the two of you. If they listen to you, you have won them over.*
> (Matthew 18:15)

If a private meeting results in being brushed off, step two becomes necessary. The offender may tell you that you have an overactive imagination. She may excuse her behavior and lash out at you for what happened. The offender may shout out their anger: "What's wrong with you?! Just get over it!" They might act as if it never really happened and you're just making a big deal out of nothing.

If the problem gets thrown back in your face in the first meeting, it's time to bring a trusted spiritual leader into the mix. This step isn't easy because you must make yourself vulnerable by telling your story without any guarantee you'll be heard or believed. Take time to fast and pray about who you will go to for help.[3] Get some wise counsel from a confidant about who you should trust to hear you out and then go with you to another private meeting.

This second meeting is Jesus' next prescribed step. Take one or two people who are strong in the faith, gifted with discernment, and guided by the Scriptures to meet face-to-face with the offender. The offense and its effect on the offended must be clear and concise without any speculation or guesses about what may or may not have happened. Stick to what you know. Every word spoken must be awash with mercy, like a graceful uncovering of the offense. This doesn't mean the insult gets whitewashed, but each word must be spoken with an attitude of readiness to forgive and an understanding that all of us are fallible beings.

If the offender's heart becomes contrite, he or she will hear you and the offense they caused will bring them to grieve. But when hardened hearts will not hear, another step must be taken to safeguard the local fellowship. Each of these steps are the love of Christ in action.

---

3. Cho Larson, "Fasting is Feasting," Chap. 19 in *Hearts for the Kingdom*. Bloomington: WestBow Press, 2015.

> *But if they will not listen, take one or two others along,*
> *so that every matter may be established by the testimony of two or three witnesses.*
> *(Matthew 18:16)*

Discipline is difficult for everyone involved. In fact, this is where being of the Church tests our mettle. Those involved in this orderly process must pray earnestly for godly wisdom, fervently intercede on behalf of the offended and offender, and take time to fast, pray, and seek the Lord to be sure God's word lights the way to truth.

The dangers of avoiding these steps of discipline are greater than the hazards in going forward. There are no guaranteed outcomes. In reality, because love is above all, we act accordingly to tackle these tough duties. This is a patient, caring, grace-filled, humbling kind of love that never fails. Compassionate application of well-ordered discipline strengthens and preserves the church. If we overlook the need to bring matters into order, the assembly becomes vulnerable to Satan's attacks and the bonds of love will be broken. This is important to understand because this next step is very challenging.

Should the offender refuse to listen to the two or three people who talked with them in private, then the whole matter ought to be presented to the church. Jesus predicted these difficulties. He warned that there would always be some tares among the wheat.[4] These "weeds" who try to disguise themselves as wheat seldom respond to being confronted even with tact, love, and mercy. "Telling it to the church" can be a very stressful and difficult means of discipline and must be used only after other avenues are exhausted.

There are many challenges in this part of the process. As an example: Confronting a person who has a charismatic personality and talks themselves up to anyone who will listen. If this is the case, an open public gathering will turn into divisive chaos and only make matters worse.

This step does not involve forcing the person to stand in front of the gathering, pointing at them, and calling them out for their sin. We're not to beat them down with pointed accusations and humiliate them. The whole purpose is to restore them to loving fellowship in the assembly. The steps to complete this action will not be the same for every situation. Local church leaders, the offender and offended, and the unique circumstances must be considered at every point of the process. The best means to fulfill this step may be to select a council of mature people from within the church to hear the matter out, offer their wise counsel, and make a final decision.

> *If they still refuse to listen, tell it to the church.*
> *(Matthew 18:17)*

---

4. Matthew 13:24–30.

The next part of this process is often difficult and painful because the offender has rejected every opportunity to turn from causing harm. Until now, they have refused all efforts. But our Lord is never quick to give up on us.

In reality, for fallible people, this is an impossible step to take. Our natural inclination is to call down fire from heaven.[5] But for Jesus, our High Priest, the purpose is to save lives, not to destroy them. Discipline is made possible by the power of the Word and the Spirit of Christ at work in and through us. We must not allow the offender any further opportunities to cause harm to anyone in your local body of faith. Our purpose is to bring them to a right standing so they may be restored to fellowship with appropriate boundaries.

The Apostle Paul teaches a very severe form of discipline. He instructed the church in Corinth to come together in Jesus' name and, in the presence of Christ, release the rebellious person to experience the consequences of their sin. Their good purpose is for the offender's sinful nature to be destroyed so he will be finally redeemed on the day of the Lord.[6]

In the past, some churches excommunicated the sinner or cancelled their membership, but these are extreme measures. Jesus taught that we should treat them like pagans and tax collectors. So, let's think about what it would be like to have someone come into our worship gathering as a heathen who works for the Internal Revenue Service. How would we treat them? How would we treat a recent divorcee? What would we do when a felon attends who just got paroled after serving ten years for assault and armed robbery? When an LGBTQ couple takes a seat next to us, how will we receive them? The answer is clear. While not condoning or affirming them in their sin, we welcome them so they can hear the truths of the Gospel.

Hearing the truth of the Word will change their hearts and bring them into grace, forgiveness, and the mercies of our Lord and Savior. Then, after they come to saving knowledge of Christ, we welcome them to be baptized and come into fellowship with us at the Lord's Table. It's as if we embrace the lost souls while holding their offenses at a distance so we will not be brought to ruin by them.

Before a newcomer hears, believes, and is brought to saving faith, they wouldn't be asked to teach a Sunday School class. They would not be placed in leadership until they have proven themselves.[7] They are welcomed to hear and receive the Good News of the kingdom of heaven, repent, and be baptized into Christ. Typically, we would treat a recalcitrant offender in the same way as a non-Christian newcomer who works for the IRS.

---

5. Luke 9:54.
6. 1 Corinthians 5:5.
7. 1 Timothy 3:10.

A person shouldn't be asked to leave a local assembly except in extreme cases. Even then, only until they have overcome their human failings that once poisoned the local gathering. We should always be ready to welcome back any lost sheep who repents and returns.

> *And if they refuse to listen even to the church,*
> *treat them as you would a pagan or a tax collector.*
> (Matthew 18:17)

Every word spoken, action taken, and judgment rendered must be awash in the love of Christ. Our objective is to bring a person the Throne of Grace[8] where they will turn around, ask for forgiveness, and be restored to the community of faith. In this way, the authority our High Priest becomes evident in our gatherings. Those who serve in an office of the Church administer justice, mercy and forgiveness as they serve under Christ's authority. This is not judgment imposed from an ivory tower upon lowly people, but a decision made in agreement with the Word, the Holy Spirit, and in the communion of saints.

The offender should not be considered an enemy, but admonished as a brother or sister in Christ. But be wise and cautious. If the offender tends to drag others down into their weaknesses, this may not be someone you want to spend time with.

The exercise of discipline in a Christian gathering must be an act saturated with prayer, administered patiently, applied in all humility, and with the good purpose of protecting the people who are the Church. Discipline's aim is to heal, reconcile, and bring the wayward soul back into the full fellowship of worship. Restoring a wandering soul and the bond of love in a local gathering is the purpose of all loving discipline. Most important of all, we must make love-driven forgiveness and mercy our foundation when it comes to rebuilding.

> *Truly I tell you, whatever you bind on earth will be bound in heaven,*
> *and whatever you loose on earth will be loosed in heaven.*
> *"Again, truly I tell you that if two of you on earth agree about anything they ask for,*
> *it will be done for them by my Father in heaven.*
> *For where two or three gather in my name, there am I with them."*
> (Matthew 18:18–20)

Church discipline is an act of endearment with a generous application of restorative love to strengthen the body of Christ. When we reprove the saints according to Gospel truth, this is like a fountain of living waters where the holy Scriptures serve as a cleansing agent. Good outcomes are only possible

---
8. Hebrews 4:16.

with much prayer, fasting, and humbling of ourselves. Some will hear, receive, and believe the Good News, while other hearts will be hardened to the words of eternal life.

In the final judgment, the weeds among the wheat, the bad fish, and the thorns in the harvest field will be sorted out, separated, and burned. It's like separating wheat from the straw and tossing chaff to the wind.[9] We must not be reluctant to administer God's loving justice among those who are called by His name. Remember that in the end it will be the saints who judge the world.[10] The work of the Church today offers us a preview of the final administration of all justice. Elders and leaders in our gatherings are called to build an atmosphere of righteousness and justice. Together, God's people make wise, godly, just, loving, and right decisions to strengthen the body of Christ—the Church. This outcropping of righteousness is possible because of the love of the Spirit of Christ at work in and through those who are called by His name.

13. Loving Discipline
Q & A

1. What is the first step of discipline Jesus taught to help those He loves?

2. If we ignore or reject discipline, what might be the consequence?

3. Why is loving, caring, tactful discipline so important in a gathering for worship?

4. Why are Jesus' progressive steps for church discipline so crucial to orderly worship?

---

9. Psalm 1:4.
10. 1 Corinthians 6:2.

My Journal Notes

Chapter 14
Perfect Love Promotes Justice

Key Scriptures:

- "I will betroth you to me forever; I will betroth you in righteousness and justice, in love and compassion." (Hosea 2:19)

- "My righteousness draws near speedily, my salvation is on the way, and my arm will bring justice to the nations. The islands will look to me and wait in hope for my arm." (Isaiah 51:5)

- "I will make justice the measuring line and righteousness the plumb line; hail will sweep away your refuge, the lie, and water will overflow your hiding place." (Isaiah 28:17)

Love without justice is a pretense—like clouds that refuse rain to a sun-scorched land. All too often in a fallen world, the seed of justice springs up in parched soil and then, in the heat of day, its struggling sprout withers away. As the new growth fades, injustice grows like a weed to push out what remains of this budding justice.

In this study, we will learn that justice holds a balancing scale to weigh right and wrong, to separate justice from injustice. We'll come to see justice as a supporting pillar for the love Christ has shown toward us. We'll learn that righteousness and justice embrace, as if braided together with the love of Christ to become like an unbreakable cord. This study will bring us to a greater knowledge of Jesus Christ, who is our advocate for the sake of love-driven justice.

The best view of justice in the Scriptures is portrayed in Jesus' own words. Those who were in the room heard Jesus speak these words and saw them fulfilled right before their eyes. Wounded souls dragged down into spiritual poverty rejoiced to hear this redemptive Good News. People imprisoned in the darkness of sin were set free. Those whose eyes were blinded by religious lies and hypocrisy were healed and made to see. The cruel taskmaster, Satan, was bound and the oppressed found liberty in Immanuel. Distressed sinners found favor in Jesus' presence. Every aspect of justice became manifested and proven in Jesus' work. He taught, healed, and delivered those bound by disease. He drove out evil spirits and released people from the clutches of wicked men—all this to reveal His love-driven justice. Christ's triumphant Jubilee[1] is still at work among us today.

---
1. See Definitions in Appendix.

The Spirit of the Lord is on me, because he has anointed me to proclaim good news to the poor. He has sent me to proclaim freedom for the prisoners and recovery of sight for the blind, to set the oppressed free, to proclaim the year of the Lord's favor.
(Luke 4:18–19)

All those who are brought into covenant agreement with Jesus find great comfort in His justice. It's delightful to come into a place of favor where our petitions are treasured, our prayers are heard and received with favor. This is a blessed dwelling with boundary lines in pleasant places.[2] God's promises take effect in our lives and our Good Shepherd is ever present with us, especially in times of trouble.[3]

By means of justice, a great separation takes place,[4] like separating sheep from goats. It's like good fish separated from the worthless. Justice in the kingdom of heaven separates light from darkness.

Those who walk blind in darkness may be shocked and dismayed when they see the hard consequences of justice. But light serves to drive back darkness and all servile fear. For God's love and justice to come to full fruition, oppressors must be thrown down. As an example: At first glance, it may seem cruel and unusual to lock away a living soul for life, or confine them in isolation. But families and communities, states and nations cannot thrive if they give free rein to those who would harm or destroy them. Those who destroy must be separated to keep us safe.

Some people claim that, because of God's loving nature, He would never cause harm to anyone. They have created a god to their own liking who is like a giant hug for all of humanity. They imagine that she's a supreme being who would never judge people, even those who are violent, oppressive, or in rebellion. By means of human reasoning, they end up redefining and even weaponizing love to destroy the truth about righteous judgments against sin. An "all is love" way of thinking causes people to deny the truth of hell, judgments against acts of sin, and the eternal consequences of rebellion.

God's love is not a New Age kind of love or a cookies and milk kind of love. It's not a love that goes to great lengths to never, ever harm even a bug on the sidewalk. Some will weaponize God's loving nature in an effort to tear down the truth about God's righteous judgments. The truth is that the redemptive love God has for sinners is not like an indulgent, irresponsible parent who excuses his child's bad behavior and never imposes consequences because he loves them so much. God's just and righteous judgments are not

---

2. Psalm 16:6.
3. Psalm 46:1.
4. Cho Larson, *Great Separations*. Bloomington: WestBow Press, 2019.

negated, but rather enhanced by His love for all humankind. God, in His redemptive love, found a way to meet the demands of holiness and righteousness by providing a way for the penalty of death to be paid on our behalf through a substitute sacrifice who is Jesus Christ, the Lamb of God.

Take time to meditate on this truth and search the Scriptures. Heaven couldn't be heavenly without God's final judgments carried out by the seven angels with seven plagues that are so fearsome and awesome. The seven bowls of God's wrath cause the unrighteous to curse at God because they suffer His judgments and are forever separated. Now look up to the multitude in heaven who are gathered together and hear them shouting for joy.

Hallelu Yah![5]
Salvation and glory and power belong to our God, for true and just are his judgments.
(Revelation 19:1–2)

The fallen nature of man and sin that entered this decaying Earth[6] are the cause of pandemics, calamities, earthquakes, and earth-scorching wildfires. But God turns these disasters around to serve a good purpose. All these adversities will work for good in the battle against the darkness of sin as we march forward to His final triumph. The world's disasters may seem cruel and harsh until we hear the great promise of Christ's ultimate victory. By means of justice and righteous judgments, the oppressors will be subjected—crushed under our feet.[7] Tormentors might be able to snuff out our lives here on Earth, but they can't steal away our eternal soul and spirit.[8]

Because of the Father's love-driven justice, we have a great and eternal hope. On that great day, there will be no more death, decay, sorrow, crying, and no more pain.[9] The old cliché, "no pain, no gain," sheds some light on the workings of justice. We suffer the effects of injustice every day of our lives because we live in a sin-ruined world. But Christ Jesus has overcome the world and we now live in great hope. Life's troubles and trials show us our need of Christ who is our ever-present help—our Lord and Savior. All who overcome in Christ can look forward to that grand and eternal hope to dwell with Christ forever and ever.

God sets the lonely in families, he leads out the prisoners with singing;
but the rebellious live in a sun-scorched land.
(Psalm 68:6)

---

5. Author's interpretation based on Paleo Hebrew.
6. Romans 8:21.
7. Romans 16:20.
8. Matthew 10:28.
9. Revelation 21:4.

Freedom is made possible by Jesus, the Prince of Peace, whose love-driven acts of justice are lavishly applied for the benefit of those who are called by His holy name. God dwells in temples that are not made by human hands and justice serves to fortify each living temple. Heaven's justice makes us secure in Christ's love toward us.

If violence, corruption, and oppression do not compel us to run to Christ as a refuge, this madness eventually results in destructive chaos and anarchy. The world's insanity and the oppressor's tyranny must be dealt with to protect those whom God has called and chosen. Inflicting just judgments against sin is like wielding a sword—the word of God that strikes down the enemies of the cross.

> *Coming out of his mouth is a sharp sword with which to strike down the nations.*
> *"He will rule them with an iron scepter."*
> *He treads the winepress of the fury of the wrath of God Almighty.*
> (Revelation 19:15)

The overwhelming nature of God's love is revealed in the record of three heavenly visitors who appeared to Abraham on their way to destroy Sodom and Gomorroah.[10] The Lord of Hosts heard the outcry against wickedness and depravity and His mighty arm moved to act with justice.

The Lord Yehovah announced through these three the arrival of Abraham and Sara's promised son on their way to deal with violence and depravity in the Jordan Valley. Their promised son foreshadowed God's only Son who would take away the sins of the world.[11] Isaac served as a living, breathing, forward-looking picture of Christ, the substitute sacrificial Lamb. The angels delivered their message and then revealed their plans to Abraham before going on their way. They planned to execute judgement and bring out the few upright people who lived there. The way this story unfolds helps us to see the Lord's long-suffering, deal-making nature. Listen as Abraham bargains:

Abraham faced them and asked, "Will you sweep away the righteous with the wicked? What if there are fifty righteous people in the city?"

The Lord replied, "If I find fifty righteous people in the city of Sodom, I will spare the whole place for their sake."

The negotiations continued until Abraham begged to speak one last time. "May the Lord not be angry, but let me speak just once more. What if only ten can be found there?"

The Lord answered, "For the sake of ten, I will not destroy it."[12]

---

10. Genesis 18; 19.
11. 1 John 2:2.
12. Genesis 18:16–33.

Heaven's messengers went on their way to the plains below, where Lot and his family lived. Yehovah's abundant mercies continued as they entered the town. The townspeople's deadly violence confronted them before they could retire for the night in Lot's house. The angelic messengers had to blind the attackers and bar the doors before they could offer the Lord's gift of mercy to Lot and his family.

The two men said to Lot,
"Do you have anyone else here—sons-in-law, sons or daughters, or anyone else in the city who belongs to you? Get them out of here, because we are going to destroy this place. The outcry to the LORD against its people is so great that he has sent us to destroy it."
(Genesis 19:12–13)

Lot negotiated with the messengers, who allowed his request. After they sent Lot safely on his way, the angels destroyed all the cities on the plain except for the small town of Zoar, where Lot had asked to go. In this Biblical account, we can see God's abundant patience and mercies at every step along the way, a life-sized picture of both sides of justice. The Lord's mercies toward those who are called and chosen, and His wrath toward those who threaten to destroy them. Abraham and Sarah received the gift of a son and we have a living picture of God's one and only Son of promise—Jesus Christ, who is our Redeemer, Savior, and Lord.

Think about how love, faithfulness, righteousness, and peace lock arms and march out to fulfill God's good purpose. It's a powerful union, brought together because the Lord is always faithful in love and righteousness. In every real-life encounter, when God's people cried out against evil, both in repentance and petition, this powerful quartet came together to accomplish a good work.

Love and faithfulness meet together; righteousness and peace kiss each other.
(Psalm 85:10)

Throughout history, many people have cried out to God because of the misery and oppression pressed upon them. The Lord heard every cry and raised up a battle standard to draw good people to His side to join Him in the war against darkness. The enslaved tribes of Israel cried out and the Great I AM raised up a deliverer in Moses. The exiled people of Babylon cried out and the Lord stirred King Cyrus' heart to help the exiles return to the land of Israel. God's people surely cried out about the abuses of the church and God raised up Martin Luther. The Spirit of Christ inspired him to nail his 95 Theses to the door of the church. Moses delivered God's holy nation from slavery, King Cyrus provided for the exiles to return home, and Luther's reformation movement remains established to our day. Every victory began with many prayers for mercy and each battle was won as the Lord of Hosts raised up a banner of love.

> *May the praise of God be in their mouths and a double-edged sword in their hands,*
> *to inflict vengeance on the nations and punishment on the peoples,*
> *to bind their kings with fetters, their nobles with shackles of iron,*
> *to carry out the sentence written against them–*
> *This is the glory of all his faithful people. Praise the LORD.*
> (Psalm 149:6–9)

Our fallible human nature tends to lead us into cycles of spiritual decline until the Lord steps in to revive and restore us by the power of His word and the work of the Holy Spirit. This is pictured in the Old Testament nation of Israel as an example to teach and warn us today. Yehovah God gave His people blessed promises to make them a holy nation and establish them in a land of their own. The people were unfaithful, but the Lord is always faithful to fulfill His promise. He blessed and prospered His people in the land. In their prosperity, they became complacent and wandered away from God. They yearned for false gods made in their own image, to their own likings, and by their own hands. The Lord God was patient with them for many years until their wickedness caused an outcry from those people who remained faithful and who grieved over the sin all around them. The violent and destructive wickedness of the unfaithful became like an avalanche that gains power as it speeds down the mountain. Their sin eventually bore the fruit of the seed they sowed and a day of justice and judgment against their horrible sins came upon them. Their evil ways caused their homeland to be conquered and the people exiled to foreign nations.

And yet, with every act of judgment, God remembered mercy. With every consequence imposed upon them, the Father purposed to bring them back home into sweet fellowship and covenant blessings. Over and over again, the people of Israel broke their covenant from the heart of God. But the God of Abraham, Isaac, and Jacob remained faithful to fulfill all His promises. God has not changed.

> *If we are faithless, he remains faithful, for he cannot disown himself.*
> (2 Timothy 2:13)

In the written histories of God's people, we can see Yehovah God's righteousness and justice come together in a loving embrace. Together, they make God's faithfulness undeniably evident. Again and again, we see love fulfilled in God's acts of righteous judgment against sin that would have forever destroyed

His people. The depth and breadth of the Lord's love is fulfilled in a covenant of love He has made with all those who are called by His holy name.

> *Righteousness and justice are the foundation of your throne;*
> *love and faithfulness go before you.*
> (Psalm 89:14)

From the very beginning, in His abundant love, God provided a remedy for fallen creation. The imprint of the cross of Jesus Christ is evident in the Word of creation. The Word called into existence things that did not exist.[13] He spoke and the sun, moon, stars, and planets came to be, and they serve to drive back the darkness.

Abraham and Sarah's promised son, Isaac, prefigured God's only Son, the Son of Promise. The Great I AM delivered His people from bondage with signs and wonders inflicted on the Egyptians to foreshadow our deliverance by the promised Messiah. The Lord manifested His saving grace again as He baptized Israel as a nation, leading them through the Red Sea. The Lord Almighty assembled the people in the wilderness and jealously protected their nation against the great warrior kings of the land. God of Israel gave Moses the design for the Tabernacle of Testimony in the wilderness as a living illustration and reminder of His grace, mercy, faithfulness, and power to save. Every element of worship in the temple pointed forward to Christ, the final sacrifice. Then, Solomon built a temple to God's holy name in Jerusalem, where the people worshiped with rites and celebrations that prefigured Christ's work of redemption.

Christ is revealed from the first words of creation: "Let there be light." From then, through the centuries, people looked forward to hear the voice of John the Baptist shouting in the wilderness: "Make straight the way of the Lord!" Every act and word spoken by the prophets pointed forward to Yeshua HaMashiach.[14] Now, we have a better covenant by means of the cross of Jesus Christ. Our Lord Jesus serves as High Priest of the church and sits at the right hand of the Father to advocate on our behalf before the Throne of Grace. He takes us under His wings. He wraps us in His robe of righteousness. He gives us favor before our heavenly Father. We have a High Priest who is our advocate. He ushers us into the presence of our God, who is King, Lord, Master, Friend, and Father—all because of His immeasurable love for those who are called by His holy name.

---

13. Romans 4:17.
14. Jesus the Anointed One.

> *Even now my witness is in heaven; my advocate is on high.*
> *My intercessor is my friend as my eyes pour out tears to God;*
> *on behalf of a man he pleads with God as one pleads for a friend.*
> (Job 16:19–21)

God's immeasurable love for all those who are called by His name is manifested on a scale of Justice where a great separation is made. The injustice of oppressors is thrown down and God's people are raised up, victorious in Christ. These overcomers are made pillars in God's holy temple.[15] They are made overcomers in Christ because His love is stronger than death,[16] and greater than faith and hope.[17] When righteousness and justice embrace, they become like an unbreakable cord to bind us together in Christ. Our Lord Jesus serves as our High Priest who is able to empathize with us in our weaknesses and failings and He serves to intercede on our behalf before the throne of grace. When we come into our Father's holy presence, we are wrapped in Jesus' robes of righteousness to present us blameless.

This is justice. It's a love-driven justice that completes God's affections toward the sheep of His pasture. But establishing and upholding an altruistic justice is hard and selfless labor—a cross that we too must take up.[18] Why else would Jesus ask if this faithful pursuit of justice would be found on earth "when the Son of Man comes"?

> *Will not God bring about justice for his chosen ones, who cry out to him day and night?*
> *Will he keep putting them off? I tell you, he will see that they get justice, and quickly.*
> *However, when the Son of Man comes, will he find faith on the earth?*
> (Luke 18:7–8)

---

15. Revelation 3:12.
16. Song of Songs 8:6.
17. I Corinthians 13:13.
18. Matthew 16:24.

14. Perfect Love Promotes Justice
Q & A

1. Describe both sides of how God's love-driven justice is revealed.

2. What is the result of an "all is love" kind of philosophy?

3. How does it change our perspective of life's suffering when we look forward to Christ's final victory?

4. How did Abraham's angelic visitors display both aspects of God's love-driven justice?

My Journal Notes:

Chapter 15
The Fragrance of Love

Key Scriptures:

- "Pleasing is the fragrance of your perfumes; your name is like perfume poured out." (Song of Songs 1:3)
- "Then Mary took about a pint of pure nard, an expensive perfume; she poured it on Jesus' feet and wiped his feet with her hair. And the house was filled with the fragrance of the perfume." (John 12:3)

Take a stroll through a vineyard as the fruit begins to ripen. The fragrance of grapes will engulf your senses. Spread a blanket to lay down in a grove of cedar trees and the aromas will enfold you as you breathe in. Stand downwind at the far corner of a field of golden grain and the gentle breezes will waft their scent over you and enfold you with their embrace. Hold a newborn child close and the special scent of the gift of life will captivate your heart.

Every one of life's special bequests has its own aroma. Every port on the islands and the continents has an identifying smell that all weathered sailors recognize. Every season of the year has its own scent: the chill of winter, the blossoms of spring, the ripening corn in your garden, and the orchard fruits ready to pick in the Autumn; all have a unique bouquet.

The gift of love the Bridegroom has for His bride and her love in return create a medley of fragrances, each in its season. The bride of Christ does well to cherish, treasure, and bask in the scents of this love. We breathe in every sweet-scented word the Lover of our souls speaks softly to us—His bride—the Church.

How delightful is your love, my sister, my bride!
How much more pleasing is your love than wine,
and the fragrance of your perfume more than any spice!

Your lips drop sweetness as the honeycomb, my bride;
milk and honey are under your tongue.

The fragrance of your garments is like the fragrance of Lebanon.
You are a garden locked up, my sister, my bride;
you are a spring enclosed, a sealed fountain.

> *Your plants are an orchard of pomegranates with choice fruits,*
> *with henna and nard, nard and saffron, calamus and cinnamon,*
> *with every kind of incense tree,*
> *with myrrh and aloes and all the finest spices.*
>
> *You are a garden fountain, a well of flowing water streaming down from Lebanon*
> (Song of Songs 4:10–15)

On the sixth day of creation, the Creator placed two beings to live in Eden. The wind of the Spirit breathed into them and man became a living soul, created in God's image. The Father's perfect love for his children, Adam and Eve, created a bond beyond anything we can imagine. Creator God walked together with His created beings in the cool of the day. Surely, they desired to walk where mandrakes sent out their fragrance.[1] Wouldn't they stop along the path to enjoy the aromas of the ripe pomegranates, cinnamon trees, henna trees, spikenard plants, and even the thorny myrrh trees? These precious aromas would certainly create memories of the Creator's love and their treasured moments together. Aromas are powerful reminders and, for the rest of their days on Earth, these scented trees must have triggered memories of the sweet moments they lost. The scents of their orchards gave them hope of a paradise restored.

The Spirit of Jesus breathes out precious words for the bride of Christ—fragrant words of affection. His breath is the four winds of the Earth that waft over the garden of the Lord[2] to carry the aromas of His affections upon those who are called by His holy name. Stop in your tracks. Stand still and be quiet for a moment. Let the chaos of the world pass you by as you breathe to receive these fragrant words of God's abundant love toward His own. Now, filled with the breath of the Spirit, God's covenant bride sings out in response to the Bridegroom's fragrances of love:

> *Awake, north wind, and come, south wind!*
> *Blow on my garden, that its fragrance may spread everywhere.*
> *Let my beloved come into his garden and taste its choice fruits.*
> (Song of Songs 4:16)

In the abundance of the garden, Adam and Eve lacked for nothing. Yet, it's as if it wasn't enough. The tempter came and enticed Eve to reach out her hand to take the forbidden fruit. Then she offered the fruit to Adam. They broke their covenant with the Creator and He banished them from this garden filled with the fragrance of the Creator's love. An angel with a flaming

---

1. Song of Songs 7:13.
2. Isaiah 51:3.

sword in hand guarded the way to the Tree of Life in the garden. But then, Father God made a way for all who would to partake of the fruit of the Vine.

The first couple's sin brought on the pain of childbirth and sweaty toil of working the land to provide food for their tables. The consequences of their fall were not only for them but for all people who would come after. But in His great love, the Creator didn't leave them or us without hope. He provided a narrow path that leads to the Tree in the Garden of God. Jesus shields us through the flames of the angel's sword so that we will not be burned.[3] Our Lord, Jesus Christ, is the narrow gate that leads us to partake of the true vine. He lights our pathway to make a way for us to triumph over the tempter by the blood of the Lamb and the word of our testimony.[4] He brings us into a fragrant garden filled with aromas of love that draw the bride to the Bridegroom's side. Our God, Father, and Creator pours out this abundant love on all those who are invited to join Him in the wedding banquet.

Will you accept His invitation to this garden wedding?

> *His splendor will be like an olive tree, his fragrance like a cedar of Lebanon.*
> *People will dwell again in his shade; they will flourish like the grain,*
> *they will blossom like the vine–Israel's fame will be like the wine of Lebanon.*
> (Hosea 14:6–7)

Is it possible that the same fragrance could be pleasant to one and repulsive to another? As an example: The aromas of hay in the barn smell like home to the son of a dairy farmer. But to kids from the city it's like, "Gag! Get me out of here!" This common illustration helps us understand this truth. Jesus proclaims Good News to the poor, freedom for the prisoners, sight for the blind, and calls for the oppressed to be set free.[5] Those with rebellion in their hearts hear these words as condemnation. Those with humble hearts hear words of eternal life.

The fragrance of the Rose of Sharon[6] is a sweet-smelling aroma to those who believe and receive His gift of saving grace. To those whose hearts remain in rebellion, the Lily of the Valley is like a stench from the grave. The very same fragrance, the same words, are the sweetness of life to those who hear and receive, but putrid to those who reject and scorn.

> *To the one we are an aroma that brings death;*
> *to the other, an aroma that brings life.*
> *And who is equal to such a task?*
> (2 Corinthians 2:16)

---
3. Isaiah 43:2–3.
4. Revelation 12:11.
5. Luke 4:18.
6. Song of Songs 2:1.

Favorable winds blow from North, South, East and West to carry the sweetness of God's love and burst our senses with delight. This is the fragrance of the Father's abundant affections for us. In this moment of God's favor, we put aside rebellion and stop to breathe in the sweet aromas of His love. In this moment, the Spirit of Jesus holds out the gift of life. The Spirit will lead us through the narrow gate to the Tree of Life who is Jesus: the Way, the Truth, and the Life.

> Our Prayer: May the sweet fragrance of His love draw us to the Throne of Grace.

15. The Fragrance of Love
Q & A

1. Describe the fragrance of God's love and what it means to you.
   _____
   _____

2. What words best describe how the Bridegroom sees His bride?
   _____
   _____

3. How is it possible for the same fragrance to be pleasant to one person and repulsive to another?
   _____
   _____

My Journal Notes:

Chapter 16
Love-Inspired Obedience

Key Scriptures:

- "If you love me, keep my commands ... Whoever has my commands and keeps them is the one who loves me." (John 14:15, 21)
- "It was good for me to be afflicted so that I might learn your decrees." (Psalm 119:71)
- "But Samuel replied: 'Does the LORD delight in burnt offerings and sacrifices as much as in obeying the LORD? To obey is better than sacrifice, and to heed is better than the fat of rams.'" (1 Samuel 15:22)

Throughout this study are many references to "delighted obedience." The truth behind this phrase is power-packed with significance for all those who abide in the kingdom of heaven. We'll focus on love-driven obedience that occurs as naturally as the sap of a grape vine flowing to the branches to produce blossoms and good fruit. All those who are grafted into Christ, the True Vine, will branch out, blossom, and produce a delightful harvest.

This study teaches why obedience is better than sacrifice. Not an obligatory obedience, but one that flows from a heart that delights in God's commands and acts in accord with Biblical precepts—because of the love in our hearts for our Lord and Savior.

A love-inspired obedience is like building a solid and safe house for our family. The foundation for a house must be level, square, and stable so the rest of the house can be built sound and solid. A foundation must never be set in a peat bog or in water-saturated, shifting sand because neither foundation nor house will stand.

Because we build for eternity, our spiritual foundation is even more important than that of a stick-framed house. The stable place for us to build a solid spiritual foundation is Christ Jesus, the Rock. Our new life in Christ is built precept upon precept, applying Scripture upon Scripture, to build a temple strong as a fortress. We build this spiritual house with love as the bonding agent. Word upon word, deed upon deed we construct a solid temple where the Spirit of Christ dwells.[1]

> *Therefore everyone who hears these words of mine and puts them into practice is like a wise man who built his house on the rock.*
> (Matthew 7:24)

---

1. 1 Corinthians 6:19.

In his letters to the seven churches, the Apostle John calls us to overcome, be victorious, and then hold on until the end so that we may reign with Christ.[2] We are called to obey Jesus' commands and the teachings of the Apostles and Prophets. The essence of this obedience is delight. We embrace the instructions they penned and the law written on our hearts. The reality for us in this world is that this righteousness is only possible in Christ.

Fallible creatures simply don't have the capacity or strength on their own to grow, mature, and be like our Lord God who is perfect.[3] As incapable mortals, we can see the beauty and mystery of the Gospel that saves us by faith in Jesus Christ. We cannot save ourselves and earth-bound humans don't have the means to perfectly obey and follow Jesus' teachings. When we see our hopeless condition, the beauty of the Good News becomes clear. Jesus the Christ, the only Son of the Living God and Savior of humankind, indwells us and He is strength, power, and might. Our Lord Jesus and all that He is dwells in us by the Holy Spirit given to us. His indwelling Spirit is our strength, and Christ Jesus is righteousness for all those who are called by His holy name. Hold fast to these truths, live in these truths, and we will continue, secure in His love.

> *If you keep my commands, you will remain in my love,*
> *just as I have kept my Father's commands and remain in his love.*
> (John 15:10)

James, the Lord's brother, wrote to the twelve scattered tribes to encourage them in their Christian faith. His letter focuses on manifestations of faith, rather than mere lip service. If James wrote to churches in modern vernacular, he might use the phrase: "Deeds above creeds." Or he might write: "Don't just ♡ Jesus on social media, put love into action."

James emphasizes the law that gives freedom, offering clear instructions for those who confess a living, active, saving faith in Jesus Christ:

1. Look with intense interest to know the perfect law that leads to freedom.
2. Do what you have learned and continue doing it.
3. Remember what you have heard by applying it to daily life.

James wraps up his instruction with a sure promise of God's blessings for those who obey. He isn't teaching that our heavenly Father's relationship with us is one that demands obedience and then He will bless us. It's more like a snowball effect. He has loved us first. We respond with love and joy, and, because of this love, we delight to obey the law written on our hearts. Our

---

2. Revelation 3:11.
3. Matthew 5:48.

love-inspired deeds bring blessings upon us—and the cycle of obedience and blessings continues to build.

> *But whoever looks intently into the perfect law that gives freedom,*
> *and continues in it–not forgetting what they have heard, but doing it–*
> *they will be blessed in what they do.*
> (James 1:25)

There is more than enough suffering in the world, but the suffering isn't just around us. These dangers affect our emotions, our mental health, our physical health, our safety, and our well-being. Chaos comes in many forms: A community in turmoil, caught up in violent protests. Once faithful church leaders who betray our trust. Those who used to love us turning against us. The co-workers we always relied on now scorning us because of our newfound faith in Jesus Christ. The home we built for our family lying in ashes after a raging wildfire. Our children taken away because of vicious lies.

Each one of these trials gives opportunity to temptations that we must pray earnestly to overcome. We're tested and tried but, when we are steeped in God's word and strengthened in our spirit, we can rule over the flesh in devoted awe of Christ Jesus. Indeed, a tried and tested character produces a shatterproof hope that will never disappoint.[4]

> *During the days of Jesus' life on earth, he offered up prayers and petitions with fervent*
> *cries and tears to the one who could save him from death, and he was heard because of*
> *his reverent submission. Son though he was, he learned obedience from what he suffered.*
> (Hebrews 5:7–8)

Love is an amazing force for good in every family, community, and nation on earth. It's like glue that holds all creation together. A godly love is as necessary to life as water is to our bodies. A newborn child who is never held, touched, or loved will not thrive. But a mother shows love to her newborn child as she changes diapers, gently bathes, feeds, and shelters her. Because of her love, she follows the laws of nature for growing a healthy and happy child.

Jesus offers Himself as an example of love-inspired obedience. He not only fulfilled the Old Testament law, but also the law of love that encompasses all the commandments. Jesus spoke only what He heard the Father speak. He touched and healed those whom the Father touched. He followed every path the Father blazed before Him. And, as He approached the end of His ministry, love drove Him toward Jerusalem where He would suffer and die in our place, for our sin.

---

4. Romans 5:3–5.

> *I love the Father and do exactly what my Father has commanded me.*
> (John 14:31)

Words of correction, imposed consequences, and painful penalties are signs of the Father's love toward those who are called by His holy name. This loving discipline has a good purpose—to turn our hearts to repentance so we can be restored to right relationship with Him. Those who have contrite hearts will be quick to repent with a little chastening. For those who persist in sin, they will need more discipline before their hearts will change.

The very best discipline plan for every one of Jesus' disciples is to first accept correction of the written word—the Bible. When we apply the holy Scriptures to our daily lives, this can be a bit painful, but less so than the consequences of our sin . Some of the most difficult pain to bear is suffering the impact of another person's wrongdoing. Whether we are disciplined for our own actions or suffer from another person's wrong, the best plan is the same—we must own it and come to the Lord with a repentant heart. We do this because we are all one in Christ.

Can you hear Jesus Christ, the Word knocking on your heart's door?

> *Those whom I love I rebuke and discipline. So be earnest and repent.*
> *Here I am! I stand at the door and knock. If anyone hears my voice and opens the door,*
> *I will come in and eat with that person, and they with me.*
> (Revelation 3:19–20)

God's loving discipline afflicts us for our own good—an eternal good. Our character is tested and tried when we are disciplined and this gives us a great and eternal hope that will never disappoint. "Because God's love has been poured out into our hearts through the Holy Spirit, who has been given to us."[5]

Samuel, Israel's judge, made an incredibly bold statement: "To obey is better than sacrifice."[6] As followers of Jesus, it is good to examine ourselves and ask, "Will I act in loving obedience, or will I once again call on Jesus' sacrifice made for my sin?"

Please remember that Jesus' sacrifice is readily available for all whose feet slip on this narrow pathway[7] and then confess their sin with a repentant heart. Our Father is quick to forgive for the sake of His holy name. Samuel's statement bears repeating for emphasis: Will we take up our cross and walk in obedience, or will we require Jesus' sacrifice for our sin? It's so much better to live in delighted obedience than to drive the nails into Jesus' hands and feet

---

5. Romans 5:5.
6. 1 Samuel 15:22.
7. Psalm 94:18.

once again by our willful sin. Yet, in every day of our lives, we all fail in what we do or don't do. In essence, we set our hearts to live in obedience and, when we sin, we have an Advocate[8] before the Father. Jesus pleads on our behalf, as if he shows His nail scarred hands, saying; "I paid the penalty for this sin. She is forgiven."

Now that we are shown mercy, forgiven and cleansed, we find security in Jesus' promises. As we continue to walk in accord with love-driven obedience, our hearts will overflow with a greater love for our Lord and Savior. The hope of our salvation becomes shatterproof because we have been disciplined and proven in the holy Scriptures and by loving reproofs from our heavenly Father.

16. Love-Inspired Obedience
Q & A

1. Define delighted obedience.

2. Why is obedience better than sacrifice?

3. Keeping God's commands and living by the law of love written on our hearts is an impossible requirement. How do we become victorious overcomers?

4. Describe how love compels us to delighted obedience.

---

8. 1 John 2:1.

My Journal Notes:

Chapter 17
Perfect Love Casts out all Fear

Key Scriptures:

- "There is no fear in love. But perfect love drives out fear, because fear has to do with punishment. The one who fears is not made perfect in love." (1 John 4:18)

- "Come, my children, listen to me; I will teach you the fear of the LORD." (Psalm 34:11)

This study's topic leads us into a dichotomy. It's an ideological clash. The call to not fear must be reconciled with the command to fear the Lord. This ambiguity is resolved when we know that God's perfect love does cast out all fear of judgment, and this freedom leads us to the fear of the Lord. Is the conflict of these contrasting fears because the right hand doesn't know what the left hand does? In this study, we'll explore this question and search the Scriptures to understand different fears and gain a clear picture of this love-inspired fear of the Lord.

In Jesus' parable of the minas, He tells a story of three servants given money to invest while their master left on a journey to be crowned king. The parable ends with the sad story of an unfaithful servant who tucks away his one mina, fearful of his Master. This servant's anxious worries were not the same as the "fear of the Lord."[1] He didn't love the master. Instead, he lived in fear of punishment. A groveling kind of fear bound him. This slave-like, self-centered fear made him unproductive. He hid away the gift given to him because of a self-focused fear in his heart. This kind of fear has its roots in the world's darkness and no part in love-inspired awe and reverence of the Lord.[2] If he sincerely loved his master, he would have esteemed Him and invested wisely.

> *I was afraid of you, because you are a hard man.*
> *You take out what you did not put in and reap what you did not sow.*
> (Luke 19:21)

When we walk in the light of day we can see where we step and we're not concerned that we will trip or stumble. When we dwell in the Almighty's stronghold, we walk in safety because our footsteps are flooded with light of the holy

---

1. Proverbs 1:7.
2. Romans 8:15.

Scriptures.[3] For those who abide in the Lord, He is our High Tower. From this high place we have light to see the dangers that surround us. The light of Christ saves us from falling into life's snares that would entrap us. This is the light of victory and the light that overcomes the darkness of this world. Because of this, we have no cause to fear any man. There is no need to grovel in front of those who would snuff out our life, because they cannot kill our eternal soul and spirit.[4]

> *The Lord is my light and my salvation–whom shall I fear?*
> *The Lord is the stronghold of my life–of whom shall I be afraid?*
> (Psalm 27:1)

Living in an age of pandemics provides us with more than enough bad news to digest. Every day, there's a new death toll to announce. In times of war, we hear a growing list of sons and daughters lost in battle. Wildfires produce reports of acres, homes, and businesses burned to ashes. As the days pass, the headlines get closer and closer to home. Every news outlet cranks out a constant stream of reports on the chaos, conflicting political opinions, and contradictory medical advice. It's as if we can feel the earth move and shake under our feet. In the blink of an eye, the world changes and what we see when we open our eyes unnerves us.

For those who are anchored in the Rock, Christ Jesus, our perspective is centered in the love of Christ—an eternal love. Even when surrounded by turmoil and chaos, we are covered in the shadow of His wings. Our Lord Jesus gathers us into a safe place like sheep in a fold. We're like fragile baby chicks gathered under His mighty wings. There is a great assurance even if we're like the fearful lamb that ran off and got lost. The Good Shepherd will come to search until He finds His lost lambs and carries them close to His heart.

> *They will have no fear of bad news; their hearts are steadfast, trusting in the Lord.*
> (Psalm 112:7)

This love-inspired fear of the Lord is manifested in everyday life as reverence, awe, and delighted obedience. Every one of us needs this kind of holy trepidation. When we get a bit of wanderlust, this healthy fear keeps our feet on the right path. The Holy Spirit opens our hearts and minds to the words of Scripture and, as we read, study, and meditate, a sense of awe washes over us. Our times of private and corporate worship are empowered as we lift up hands in reverence to His holy name. This is the fountain that springs up to refresh us with life-giving waters; a lifesaving flow that offers the wisdom of Christ to keep us from the traps that would seize us.

---

3. Psalm 119:105.
4. Matthew 10:28.

The fear of the LORD is a fountain of life, turning a person from the snares of death
(Proverbs 14:27)

    Earth's privation or abundance are not the weights and measures used in the Kingdom of Heaven. The world's measure is a bank account balance. The neighbors may assess us based on the car parked in our driveway. But even 1,000,000 zeros in an investment account add up to zero in the realm of God's kingdom. In fact, because of our inclination for self-dependency, we're better off in this life to have just enough tea in our cup,[5] with a heaping spoonful of the fear of the Lord stirred in for sweetness. Our love of Christ compels us to store up treasure in heaven where no one can steal it. When our treasures are stored in heaven's vault, we can enjoy a peaceful life of restful faith that compels us to pray with confidence every day: "Give us this day our daily bread."

Better a little with the fear of the LORD than great wealth with turmoil.
(Proverbs 15:16)

    There is no conflict between these dissimilar fears. Those who live in fear of judgment have yet to know the love of Christ. Those who love the Lord with all their hearts will walk in the fear of the Lord—in reverence, awe, and delighted obedience. When we are wrapped in the Good Shepherd's loving arms, we have no need to fear anything that might come against us. Neither pandemics, earthquakes, nor wildfires will be cause for fear because we walk in a love-inspired fear of the Lord. Even while winds batter and shake our home, we can rest assured in the love of Christ and lift up holy hands to worship, serve, and minister. When the doors of a church lock us out, we can still overflow with thanksgiving, praise, and worship before a holy God with Christ Jesus who serves as our High Priest. The Church is not built with brick and mortar. Whether in poverty or abundance, whatever state we're in, we can know God's perfect love that casts out all fear.

---

5. Proverbs 30:8–9.

17. Perfect Love Casts Out all Fear
Q & A

1. What is servile fear and why is it so destructive?

2. Describe the fear of the Lord.

3. How do treasures we store up in heaven help us to live free from fear of life's calamities?

My Journal Notes:

Chapter 18
Love is a Banner

Key Scriptures:

- "Let him lead me to the banquet hall, and let his banner over me be love." (Song of Songs 2:4)

- "This is what the Lord God says: Look, I will lift up my hand to the nations, and raise my banner to the peoples. They will bring your sons in their arms, and your daughters will be carried on their shoulders." (Isaiah 49:22 CSB)

We're offered a delightful image that reveals God's love as a banner over us. This study will help us see the beauty of this banner and its good purpose. We'll learn that it's a battle standard to declare the Lord who is mighty in battle, who will rise up and show Himself strong to fight on behalf of those He loves. This standard is unfurled in the wind of the Spirit to show His love for those who are called by His holy name. In fact, this flagstaff reveals a love for us that is beyond measure. God sent His only Son to die in our place, for our sin. This is the greatest act of love and this love covers us as a banner. They raised our Lord Jesus as a standard on a hilltop where He gave His life blood to redeem us, and to gather us in love as His own.[1]

When Yehovah God brought the tribes of Israel out of slavery in Egypt, He covered them. In the daytime, He sheltered them with a pillar of cloud. Through the night, He covered them with light from a column of fire. Whether day or night, as long as the cloud or fire moved, the people could travel. With abundant love for His chosen people, He protected them from the burning heat of day and drove back the darkness of night. As God's holy nation trekked through the wilderness, they pitched their tents when the cloud settled and they pulled up their tent stakes to move out when the cloud moved.

Each of the twelve tribes held up a unique banner as a sign for their people to gather. Trumpets would sound and, with banners raised, the tribes rallied and prepared to move out. The leaders for the tribe of Judah lifted up their standard to draw their people together, and then they led the way for eleven tribes to follow. Judah lifted their banner of love to lead the nation. This banner prefigured Yeshua HaMashiach, our Lord Jesus Christ, the promised one who is raised up from the tribe of Judah to redeem all nations from sin's death penalty.

---

1. John 12:32.

*In that day the Root of Jesse will stand as a banner for the peoples;
the nations will rally to him, and his resting place will be glorious.*
(Isaiah 11:10)

The Mosaic Law, given to Israel, served as a banner of love to cover them. This same ensign warned covenant violators of God's just and righteous judgments. Like a mighty Prince with his standard bearer at his side, He struck fear in the hearts of God's enemies. This flagstaff, when lifted, rallied the troops to come together and be heartened in the struggle against the forces of darkness that came against them. With the sound of a trumpet and the ensign raised, the Lord of the armies of heaven called them to armor up with sword and shield in their hands. This banner is still raised in our day to strike fear in the hearts of the God's enemies, for the Lord of Hosts is mighty in battle. All those who will hear, respond to the trumpet call, and gather around His banner find safety and comfort while God's enemies are thrown into confusion.

The covenant Moses declared between Mount Gerizim and Mount Ebal revealed Yehovah God's love for His chosen nation. The mountain where he proclaimed blessings stands higher than the mountain of curses proclaimed against those who would be rebellious of heart. The higher mountain is the greater to illustrate God's abundant grace and mercy. The Lord's Ark of the Covenant remained between the people as they stood on the side of Mount Gerizim where blessings and protection were proclaimed. As he looked toward Mount Ebal, Moses declared severe consequences for any who would refuse to follow Yehovah's covenant from the heart. One covenant served to bless those who honored God's statutes, and to warn of the consequences for those who would violate it. The blessings of love would compel them to keep the covenant, while consequences were given to turn rebellious hearts back under the protection of God's banner of love.

*All you people of the world, you who live on the earth, when a banner is raised on the
mountains, you will see it, and when a trumpet sounds, you will hear it.*
(Isaiah 18:3)

Clear the way, swing open the city gates, ascend to the highest hill, and raise up a flagstaff to call all people to be made citizens of God's holy nation. This banner is the catalyst for God's people to take their sons in their arms and daughters on their shoulders to bring them home in great celebration.[2] This banner is raised to strengthen the weak, heal wounded souls, make the lame to walk, and create a clear path for them to come to Zion's gates. Stand up and shout out to all who will hear: "Come, all you temples of the Holy

---
2. Isaiah 49:22.

Spirit from every tribe, nation, people, and culture. Let us gather to worship the Lord in all holiness—in spirit and truth. Now, enter through the gates and let us celebrate with the Bridegroom who rejoices with His bride." This is the banner of love that covers all who are in Christ.

> *Pass through, pass through the gates! Prepare the way for the people.*
> *Build up, build up the highway! Remove the stones.*
> *Raise a banner for the nations.*
> (Isaiah 62:10)

The watchmen on the walls of the city shouted out when they saw the troops returning with a banner raised to lead their procession. A victorious army came home to parade through the streets led by their Prince and His standard bearer. The children danced in the streets. Youths sang a song of triumph, and brides-in-waiting wept with joy while victorious troops gave good gifts to the people from their plunder.[3] The troops in formation with their polished weapons and armor made a beautiful sight for all those who watched earnestly for their safe return. Their army crushed those who attacked God's people. They overthrew the enemy and now it is time for great joy and celebration. This is the victory of Christ who is our banner of love and it is beautiful in every way.

> *You are as beautiful as Tirzah, my darling, as lovely as Jerusalem,*
> *as majestic as troops with banners.*
> (Song of Songs 6:4)

A liberated people will overflow with songs of praise, for their Redeemer has raised a mighty arm to save them. He raised up a banner on a hill called Golgotha[4] to gather a remnant of His people. And now, the gathered Church can rejoice as we draw water from the wells of salvation. His holy name is exalted as the people sing to the Lord, who in abundant love has done glorious things on behalf of those who are called by His holy name.

> *"There will be a highway for the remnant of his people"*
> (Isaiah 11:16)

Picture a bride dressed in white, adorned with precious jewels given as gifts of love from the one to whom she is promised. She is ushered through the garden gate with a banner held above the entrance as a declaration of the groom's love for her. Then, she waits to hear the shout: "The bridegroom is coming."

---

3. Ephesians 4:8.
4. Mathew 27:33.

The sons and daughters of the Most High God are the bride of Christ. We are the ones He loved first, so that we may now love Him and delight in obeying Him.[5] This love is possible because God's only Son was lifted as a banner on a hill outside of Jerusalem and all who will believe and receive are drawn to gather before the cross. Our hearts, once crushed with grief over our own sinfulness, are blessed to hear those awesome words of forgiveness: "Come unto me."[6] In the joy of our faith, we act in obedience, we believe, and we are baptized.[7] Every day of our lives, from the first blink of our eyes in the morning until we close our eyes to rest for the night, we look up to where our help comes from.[8] We look to the cross of Jesus Christ as a banner on a hill to cover us in Christ's immeasurable love.

Chapter 18. Love is a Banner
Q & A

1. Give examples from the Bible of God's love displayed as a banner.

2. What purpose did a king's banner serve in ancient times?

3. Describe God's banner of love that covers His people even today.

4. What great and eternal hope does God's banner of love offer you?

---

5. 1 John 4:19.
6. Isaiah 1:18.
7. Acts 2:38.
8. Psalm 121.

My Journal Notes:

Chapter 19
Love That Separates to Make Us Inseparable

Key Scriptures:

- "For Christ's love compels us, because we are convinced that one died for all, and therefore all died." (2 Corinthians 5:14)
- "Who shall separate us from the love of Christ? Shall trouble or hardship or persecution or famine or nakedness or danger or sword?" (Romans 8:35)

No worldwide pandemic, no economic disaster, no devastating financial loss, nor any violent act against God's people can ever separate us from the love of Christ. If we could hide in the deepest ocean or travel to the furthest planet in the universe, we could not be separated from the love poured out upon us by our Lord Jesus. It's impossible to separate what has been melded together because love is stronger than death. This is the treasure of truth we will delve into in this study session, so that we may know the sure promise of God's abundant love that makes us inseparable from our Lord and Savior, Jesus Christ.

When we see our neighbor suffer after losing his job, we grieve with them. When a family gets evicted, we stand with them, distressed because of their circumstances. When whole communities are destroyed by raging wildfires, a sickened grief sweeps over us at the horror of it. Earthquake-caused tsunamis wash away schools, livelihoods, homes, and entire families. These disasters cause our hearts to mourn with those who have lost so much. And yet, we don't grieve as if we are a people without hope, because we cannot be separated from God's love.

Brothers and sisters, we do not want you to be uninformed about those who sleep in death, so that you do not grieve like the rest of mankind, who have no hope.
(1 Thessalonians 4:13)

Jesus' vicarious death and resurrection become a living reality for all those who call on the name of the Lord. The resurrection power of our crucified Messiah is an effective element of our everyday lives. We can pinch our arms to know we still have a living body, but now our flesh is crucified with Christ—we are a living sacrifice.[1] Our crucified body is still earthbound, but this mortal being no longer rules over us. Because of the power of resurrection that lives in us, we are set free from the law of sin and death.

---

1. Romans 12:1.

This is the triumph of saving grace. By faith we are united with Christ in His death and we are raised triumphant from the grave. This is the power and reality of baptism. In water and by the word of God we are made to die and be buried with our Lord Jesus, and then we are raised up with Christ in the power of resurrection. We still live in a mortal body, but the flesh no longer rules over us. Instead, our human nature is overruled by the Spirit and the Word who reign in our soul and spirit. This is the power and effect of the love that drove our Lord Jesus to the cross on our behalf.

I have been crucified with Christ and I no longer live, but Christ lives in me. The life I now live in the body, I live by faith in the Son of God, who loved me and gave himself for me.
(Galatians 2:20)

For all who remain in Christ's love,[2] our grief is sated with eternal hope. We have died with Christ and now we stand with Him in the power of resurrection. As partakers of the Bread of Life and the Cup of Covenant, we have a great and eternal hope. Even in times that seem hopeless, we can hold fast to the greatest of hope. For those who are in Christ, even the threat of death is no cause to fear.

Acts chapter 7 provides us with a record of Stephen, who was stoned to death by the religious stalwarts of his day. They grated their teeth in a furious rage as they prepared to drag him away and stone him because of his testimony about their Messiah, whom they had crucified. The mob began to lunge at him and, in that moment, Stephen looked up and said: "I see heaven open and the Son of Man standing at the right hand of God."[3] We can stand in Stephen's sandals and say, "What can mere mortals do to me?" This great confidence comes from knowing we are held secure in the hollow of His loving hands—forever.

*The L*ORD *is with me; I will not be afraid. What can mere mortals do to me?*
(Psalm 118:6)

With our feet firmly set on the planet Earth and our hearts set to store up eternal treasures in heaven, we are encompassed in God's timeless love. This love is shown to us with every morning sunrise that announces God's renewed mercies. We've repented of yesterday's failures to put them behind us, forgiven and overcome. The person we used to be is gone because we are a new creation in Christ Jesus. We have received the gift of saving faith, been obedient in baptism, and we are now raised up with Christ to be seated with Him according to the promise of entering God's eternal rest.

---

2. John 15:9.
3. Acts 7:56.

> *But because of his great love for us, God, who is rich in mercy, made us alive with Christ even when we were dead in transgressions–it is by grace you have been saved.*
> *And God raised us up with Christ and seated us with him in the heavenly realms in Christ Jesus.*
> (Ephesians 2:4–6)

Too many Christians have claimed, "Jesus did it all, so now I don't have to do anything." Some have even declared misguided words about Christ: "It doesn't matter what I do." Yes, it's true that Jesus' sacrifice, giving his body to be broken and shedding His blood as He was crucified, is completely sufficient for our salvation. It is also true that we cannot do enough good things to earn our salvation. But these flippant claims are half-truths that could lead us to deceive ourselves. The love that compelled Jesus toward Jerusalem where He would be crucified is the same love He has planted in our hearts. This is the awesome love that compels us to live according to His commands—what we do is a matter of love.

This same love floods our hearts like a fountain of life and causes us to overflow with delighted obedience. When we fail to live in accord with the One who loved us first, and we all do fail, our hearts will be struck with grief that we have offended our first Love—our Lord Jesus Christ.[4] When we break our covenant of love with Christ, our hearts will break with grief and we will run to the Throne of Grace with repentant hearts to receive His forgiveness and mercy. When we continue to walk on this path, we are separated from the chains of sin so we can continue on, secure in the love of Christ.

> *If you keep my commands, you will remain in my love,*
> *just as I have kept my Father's commands and remain in his love.*
> (John 15:10)

Loving the Lord our God with all our heart, soul, and mind is possible because our Savior has planted His love in our hearts. This is the love that embraces our neighbors, our family, and those with whom we gather to worship. Because He first loved us, we are able to love even the unlovable. Jesus' command is the law of love that He fulfilled and is now at work in our hearts. It's a sacrificial love, and its full effect is earthshaking. It will change the world around us. When this love shines out to every corner of the Earth, every tribe, nation, and culture will come under its powerful light to drive out all injustice, poverty, and prejudice.

> *My command is this: Love each other as I have loved you.*
> (John 15:12)

---

4. Revelation 2:4.

The power of love that drove Jesus to press on toward Jerusalem where He would be betrayed, arrested, falsely accused, mocked, beaten, spit upon, His beard ripped out, a crown of thorns pressed onto His head, whipped with a cat-of-nine-tails, and then nailed to a wooden cross to suffer and die—this is the greatest love ever known. Jesus gave Himself for this great purpose: to break the stranglehold death once had on us.[5] Now, in Christ, we are made inseparable from His love. He gathers all those who are called by His holy name to gather at the spring of living water that flows like a river from the throne of God. No calamity, no raging wildfire, no epidemic, and no shaking of Earth's fault lines can separate us from God's eternal, all-encompassing love.

19. Love That Separates to Make us Inseparable.
Q & A

1. How do we live as a sacrifice before the Lord Almighty?

2. How does the power of Resurrected Christ empower our lives?

3. What is it that separates us to make us inseparable from Christ?

---

5. Hebrews 2:14.

My Journal Notes:

Chapter 20
A Love that Gathers

Key Scriptures:

- "Save us, LORD our God, and gather us from the nations, that we may give thanks to your holy name and glory in your praise." (Psalm 106:47)

- "Do not forget to show hospitality to strangers, for by so doing some people have shown hospitality to angels without knowing it." (Hebrews 13:2)

God's love is a gathering love. His heart is that of a Father who opens His arms to His children. The Good Shepherd gathers His sheep like a flock in a pasture, then shelters them in a sheepfold to be safe when night hunters are on the prowl. The Great I AM gathered and encompassed Israel as a nation. The Lord God gathers His people to celebrate His holy name in worship. And at the end of time, trumpets will sound for the great and final gathering.[1] This is the love we will grasp hold of in this study.

In our day and time, God's love continues to do its incredible work in all those who are called by His holy name. His love at work in us generates a yearning for gatherings of faith. Because we are sons and daughters of the Most High God, we gather hungry souls around our table to enjoy the blessings of food and fellowship.

> *For I was hungry and you gave me something to eat, I was thirsty and you*
> *gave me something to drink, I was a stranger and you invited me in,*
> *I needed clothes and you clothed me, I was sick and you looked after me,*
> *I was in prison and you came to visit me.*
> (Matthew 25:35–36)

The Apostle John teaches a victorious faith, an overcoming faith, and a communion of faith that binds us together in love. For all who believe that Jesus is the Son of God, this love is a catalyst to delight in following the law of love planted in our hearts by the Spirit of Christ. This command is seeded in our hearts to sprout up and bear the fruit of righteousness. While we remain joined together in Christ, the True Vine, we will bear the same fruit of our victorious Savior who overcame the world on our behalf.[2] By faith, we believe and receive this great salvation. In the waters of baptism, we are joined with Christ in His death and raised up as victors in our resurrected Savior.

---

1. 1 Corinthians 15:52.
2. John 16:33.

The Apostle John referred to himself as "the one Jesus loved."[3] He wasn't placing himself in an exclusive club. Every disciple who is called by Jesus' name ought to be so familiar with His loving kindness that we can refer to ourselves as a disciple Jesus loves. This knowledge alone will spur us to love and obey Him even more. All those who are victorious in Christ will be lifted up by the wind of the Spirit to gather and strengthen each other in the bond of this awesome love.

> *"In fact, this is love for God: to keep his commands.*
> *And his commands are not burdensome, for everyone born of God overcomes the world.*
> *This is the victory that has overcome the world, even our faith.*
> *Who is it that overcomes the world?*
> *Only the one who believes that Jesus is the Son of God.*
> (1 John 5:3–5)

The loneliest, most crushing moments of life can come over us even when we are alone in a crowd. The people around us are neighbors, couples, friends, and associates—all in a buzz as they go about their business. But we feel invisible, ignored, or even shunned. They make it clear that we are not one of them. They push us aside, take advantage of us, and cheat us at every opportunity because they are stronger and we are a stranger.

But the love of Christ is contrary to the crowd. Instead, we welcome the newcomer and get to know them and their needs. We are called to protect the outsider and treat them fairly. As we serve, it's good to remember the days when we were an alien without family or friends. We know what we needed then, and now we can empathize and reach out to a new person. We are called to lead them to gather together with us in Jesus' name.

> *Do not mistreat or oppress a foreigner, for you were foreigners in Egypt.*
> (Exodus 22:21)

The day approaches when our Lord Jesus Christ will return to gather us in that great final harvest. Because that time is so near, we are called to earnestly pray for all righteousness to be fulfilled. Our prayers serve as a covering of love, like a prayer mantle spread over those for whom we pray. Our love-focused prayers cover our neighbors and their faults. Our love-centered petitions unite us and draw us to gather for fellowship in Jesus' holy name.

The prayers of the saints strengthen us in the ministry and service of spiritual gifts to all those in need of Christ. Jesus, our High Priest, calls us to ascend and gather for worship, and there we find opportunity to serve according to the good gift the Holy Spirit has empowered in us. In faithful love, we

---

3. John 20:2.

worship together in spirit and truth to make known God's abundant grace in keeping with the gifts given to us as the Spirit determines.

> *The end of all things is near.*
> *Therefore be alert and of sober mind so that you may pray. Above all, love each other deeply, because love covers over a multitude of sins. Offer hospitality to one another without grumbling. Each of you should use whatever gift you have received to serve others, as faithful stewards of God's grace in its various forms.*
> (1 Peter 4:7–10)

All those who are called by Jesus' name ought to have the mind of Christ.[4] This is possible because of the law of love written on our hearts. With this loving mindset, we come to delight in serving those in need. We make sure the needs of our own family are met, as are those of neighbors who lack life's essentials.. A family that fled abject poverty and oppression in a foreign land matters to us. Those who are impoverished, sick, or trampled down are lifted up and treated as a neighbor.

A great sin of Sodom's people was their disregard for the poor and needy.[5] The people of the Jordan Valley were overfed, arrogant, and indifferent to the needs of others. The Apostle Paul refers to people like this, who claim Jesus' name but have a selfish attitude, as "worse than unbelievers."[6]

> *If any of your fellow Israelites become poor and are unable to support themselves among you, help them as you would a foreigner and stranger, so they can continue to live among you.*
> (Leviticus 25:35)

In his letter to the Romans, Paul describes what sincere love looks like in real life. This is a love that separates like a double-edged sword. A sincere love cuts off what is evil in order to make way for righteousness to thrive. When malice is cut away, a loving environment will flourish along with a fervent affection for our neighbors. With a love that is in accord with all truth, we are zealous for the work of the Great Commission that can only be accomplished in the power and strength of the Spirit. The love of Christ works godliness in our hearts to strengthen us with the joy of the Lord.[7]

When we consider what the love of Christ accomplishes in us, we realize that righteousness is impossible apart from our Lord Jesus. Can any mortal always be filled with joy and hope? Can fallible people always be patient even when everything possible goes wrong? Do we always remember to pray even

---

4. 1 Corinthians 2:16.
5. Ezekiel 16:49.
6. 1 Timothy 5:8.
7. Nehemiah 8:10.

when prayers are desperately needed? Isn't our natural tendency to hold on too tight to what we have, rather than holding it in an open hand to share with our neighbor? After we put in sixty hours teaching kids who don't want to learn, grading papers, and dealing with school administrators, we just want to crash and binge on some mindless TV show without a thought for anybody else.

What Paul describes is humanly impossible. If we attempt to do what Christ's love calls for on our own, we will eventually burn out and give up. Instead, we must rest, bound together in His abundant love. Then, the fruit of this love manifests itself as we gather together to serve in Jesus' name.

Love must be sincere. Hate what is evil; cling to what is good. Be devoted to one another in love. Honor one another above yourselves. Never be lacking in zeal, but keep your spiritual fervor, serving the Lord. Be joyful in hope, patient in affliction, faithful in prayer. Share with the Lord's people who are in need. Practice hospitality.
(Romans 12:9–13)

The Spirit of Christ plants a love in our hearts that overflows to our neighbors. Jesus uses our outstretched arms as His own. When someone puts us down because of our faith in Jesus as Savior, we bless them in Jesus' name. When our neighbor loses her dear mother, we hold her and mourn with her. When a neighbor becomes engaged, it's an opportunity to celebrate with them. When our neighbor's messy tree branches grow out over our nice, neat lawn, we talk to them and come to an agreement. When the neighbor who works as a garbage truck driver comes home smelling bad, we treat them as our equal..

The Apostle Paul teaches us the imperatives of a godly life. It's good to remember that what he presents is not a moralistic mandate. Instead, these good deeds blossom and come to fruit when we remain grafted into the True Vine, Christ Jesus. Like a branch that draws its fluids and nutrients from the main trunk, those who are grafted into Christ will blossom and grow the fruit of the Spirit of Jesus. This is the power and effect of the law of love that grows and flourishes in our hearts. This good fruit is the bountiful harvest that draws us together in celebrative worship and thanksgiving.

Bless those who persecute you; bless and do not curse. Rejoice with those who rejoice; mourn with those who mourn. Live in harmony with one another. Do not be proud, but be willing to associate with people of low position. Do not be conceited.
(Romans 12:14–16)

What is in our hearts will inevitably be expressed in our words and actions toward others. People who are in Christ are outcroppings of all He is, so they spontaneously produce fruit in harmony with righteousness. It's important for us to see real-life examples of people who live, serve, worship, and minister in the fullness of Christ.[8] While His love is perfected in our hearts, it is good for us to follow the example of someone who lives in keeping with repentance and in agreement with their baptism into Christ.

When we die to ourselves, our personal ambitions, our likes and preferences no longer take precedence over other people's needs. Our words and deeds are a reflection of Christ who lives in us and through us. This is a unifying, gathering kind of love. Through it, we are called to live like Paul and like the godly spiritual leaders in our worship assemblies.

When our leaders fail, and they all do at some point and to some degree, their repentant attitude leads us all to see our need of Christ's mercy, grace, and forgiveness. We know when someone is ready for leadership if they are inclined to gather people around a table or get folks together for fellowship. If not, there's a good chance they're not prepared to lead in a local gathering of faith.

> *Rather, he* [an elder] *must be hospitable, one who loves what is good, who is self-controlled, upright, holy and disciplined.*
> (Titus 1:8)

When Jesus saw the crowds coming to Him, he said to His disciples, "The harvest is plentiful but the workers are few."[9] In His great love, Jesus gathered those who were needy, spiritually impoverished, sick, and lame. He set people free from bondage to demons and raised to life the precious souls of those who had died. Jesus showed us a victorious love that unifies people. His love is the impulse for forgiveness. Immanuel's prayers cover us under the wings of His prayer shawl. In love and compassion, He spoke to and blessed foreigners, Samaritans, tax collectors, and lepers alike. As He hung, nailed to a crude wooden cross, His love spoke to the repentant thief: "Truly I tell you, today you will be with me in paradise."[10]

Jesus' abundant and immeasurable love is planted in our hearts so that we may love as He loved. We can rest assured that Jesus' abundant, forgiving love covers a multitude of sins, and all repentant sinners. This affection unifies us and draws us into harmonious fellowship in Jesus' name. Our spiritual leaders serve to bring us together with Christ-like leadership. They serve their families and God's people, emulating Christ Jesus as a shepherd who holds the lambs close to his heart.

---

8. Philippians 3:17.
9. Matthew 9:37.
10. Luke 23:43.

This immeasurable love produces a bountiful harvest for God's holy angels to gather in their arms. Like plentiful grapes from the vine, like sheaves of wheat in the field, the angels will gather the beautiful fruit of love that is made possible because of the law of love He has written on our hearts.

20. A Love that Gathers
Q & A

1. What motivates a Christian's yearning to gather and worship?

2. How does the love of Christ change our life's priorities and purpose?

3. What does sincere love look like in everyday life?

4. What is the power and effect of the law of love planted in our hearts?

My Journal Notes:

Chapter 21
A Love Psalm

Key Scriptures:

- "May your unfailing love come to me, LORD, your salvation, according to your promise; then I can answer anyone who taunts me, for I trust in your word. Never take your word of truth from my mouth, for I have put my hope in your laws. I will always obey your law, for ever and ever. I will walk about in freedom, for I have sought out your precepts. I will speak of your statutes before kings and will not be put to shame, for I delight in your commands because I love them. I reach out for your commands, which I love, that I may meditate on your decrees." (Psalm 119:41–48)

- "The Spirit of the LORD will rest on him—the Spirit of wisdom and of understanding, the Spirit of counsel and of might, the Spirit of the knowledge and fear of the LORD—and he will delight in the fear of the LORD." (Isaiah 11:2–3)

The longest chapter in the Bible may also be one of the greatest love songs ever written. It is composed as confirmation of a covenant, like a salted kiss. Indeed, we have a covenant that is preserved as if with salt. In this Psalm, we see expressions of childlike trust, delighted obedience, and unshakeable faith; all inspired by the precepts, laws, promises, and decrees in the holy Scriptures. The prophet Ezra wrote by divine inspiration from a heart that overflowed with confident assurance of God's loving kindness and mercy. In this study, each segment is like one stanza in a love song. Every word, command, precept, statute and admonition expresses whispers of love and affection to all who have the greatest commandment and the second commandment which is like the first, written on our hearts.

The prophet portrays a devotion like that of a boy who loves his daddy so much that he tries to walk like him and talk in a voice like his. The child imitates his father's expressions and gestures and he steps wherever dad's big boots leave a footprint. He wears the same kind of hat and picks up tools to use them just like daddy. But when the boy hurries along to keep up and stumbles, daddy stops to pick him up, dusts him off, and sets him on his feet. This is the life of all those who have childlike faith. We are eager to walk in Jesus' footsteps, confident in His grace, forgiveness, and cleansing.

Our Lord Jesus lived in the light of this psalm as He walked the dusty roads in the ancient land of Israel. His every footstep was a step of delighted obedience. And now, we who are in Christ can walk in His sandals—in His righteousness that He credits to us. Jesus' delighted pursuit of righteousness is the seed of our desire to live in the light—in agreement with the law of love. God's banner of love serves to cover and protect us. This is the banner on a bare hilltop that beckons us to enter the kingdom's gates with joy.[1] His banner musters an army, armored up for battle—a mighty multitude who shout for joy in victory and lift up their banner in the name of the Lord.[2]

Jesus fulfilled the Law chiseled in stone and now the Holy Spirit writes the greatest commandments on our hearts.[3] Both the law written in stone and the law inscribed on our hearts have their genesis in the words spoken to bring into being all of God's creation. The same Word of creation is the foundation upon which both are established. Justice and righteousness, judgment and mercy were instituted by the Word of Creation. God's saving grace is made evident in the power and effect of the law of love in our hearts. The power of the Gospel redeems, made possible by the greatest act of love the world has ever known.[4] The Gospel is supreme because Christ's mercy overrules judgement. His mercies inspire a delighted obedience in us because the law of love is planted in our hearts. This immeasurable sacrificial love of our Lord Jesus Christ is the core truth of the Gospel.

> *This is the covenant I will establish with the people of Israel after that time, declares the Lord. I will put my laws in their minds and write them on their hearts. I will be their God, and they will be my people.*
> (Hebrews 8:10)

In his alphabetic acrostic,[5] the prophet Ezra builds, stanza by stanza, to reveal knowledge of God's love that works to affect a faith-inspired, delighted obedience in us. This psalmist builds up to a great crescendo in the last verse, where he shows us a sheep who strayed. The lamb calls out for the Good Shepherd to come and search for him because his wooly back got caught in a thorn bush. Even though he wandered and lost his way, he remembers God's commands and they become more treasured in his heart than ever before.[6] The rescued sheep is shown compassion and mercy as a wanderer who has shown a heart of forgiveness and mercy toward his neighbor.

---

1. Isaiah 13:2.
2. Psalm 20:5.
3. Matthew 22:34–40.
4. John 15:13.
5. Psalm 119.
6. Psalm 119:176.

> *For judgment is without mercy to one who has shown no mercy.*
> *Mercy triumphs over judgment.*
> (James 2:13 ESV)

A good way to love our neighbors is to be ready when they ask, "Why are you always so hopeful?" Neighbors get to know us through years of borrowed and loaned garden tools. They watch as we raise our kids, rush off to the emergency room, dress up for weddings, and mourn for loved ones lost. They put up with us when they're downwind from our backyard BBQ smoke. Our lives have shined out with the light of Christ in our neighborhood, and they watched to see how we lived. When the opportunity presents itself, we can add life-giving words to our living witness.

In these special moments, we can speak out with confidence. We can be certain of our testimony because our character has been tested and tried. With proven character, we can speak with full assurance of the hope that springs up from within us. We drank from the living waters that Jesus held out to us, and now our fountain overflows with the goodness of his saving grace and mercies to neighbors who will hear. Whether they receive or reject our words, whether they become better friends or decide to ignore us, the law of love in our hearts has spoken out with life-giving words and the Holy Spirit will complete the good work in their heart.

> *Always be prepared to give an answer to everyone who asks you to give the reason for the hope that you have. But do this with gentleness and respect, keeping a clear conscience, so that those who speak maliciously against your good behavior in Christ may be ashamed of their slander.*
> (1 Peter 3:15–16)

What is in our hearts is expressed in so many ways: our body language, the words we speak, how we respond to authority, the remarks we blurt out in anger, and our conversations over the backyard fence. The words we speak overflow from what is in our hearts. What we believe about the Lord Jesus Christ marks our words, gives nuance to our conversations, and seasons what we say in every conversation.

Some people talk too much to cover up what is really in their hearts, but their excessive words serve as a red flag to warn of what is hidden there.[7] If we listen to what people say, we can know their hearts. When we hear a wise, old saint speaking, we hear graceful words that flow up from a deep-seated faith. With hearts joined together in the same spirit of faith, we can hear words of wisdom and our conversations will mutually encourage and

---
7. Proverbs 14:3.

strengthen us. A fire is ignited when the Spirit of Christ burns bright in our hearts, and our hearts will burn to speak out with words of life, love, grace, and mercy.

> *It is written: "I believed; therefore I have spoken."*
> *Since we have that same spirit of faith, we also believe and therefore speak.*
> (2 Corinthians 4:13)

The Apostles wrote many love letters to the churches. They penned these epistles to lovingly admonish the saints and encourage them to grow in grace and knowledge.[8] They inspired God's people to love one another. They taught Jesus' followers that without love, the gifts of the Holy Spirit are little more than an irritating noise.[9] They wrote to reveal the Gospel of Christ Jesus who fulfilled the law. They penned words of Christ so they could stand fast, unscathed by the condemnation of the Law.[10] The Apostles encouraged Christ's followers to unleash the law of love written in their hearts because love's good fruit testifies of the true grace of God at work among them.[11] They taught the people to know the freedom they found in Christ: liberty to live in Christ, and to walk in His footsteps.[12] Every word they wrote revealed Christ, the Rock where their feet would find a sure footing.

> *With the help of Silas, whom I regard as a faithful brother,*
> *I have written to you briefly, encouraging you and testifying that this is the true grace of God.*
> *Stand fast in it.*
> (1 Peter 5:12)

When we pass through the fires of adversity, our character is tried, tested, and refined. When our character is honed and proven according to faith, a great and eternal hope is kindled in our hearts. This hope builds like a fire in our bones, ready to burst out of our mouths like a fiery sword—the sword of the Spirit which is the word of God. This is the fire of love, and we will become worn-out should we try to hold it in.

We shout out to friends and neighbors about the greatest moments in our lives: a baby born into our family, a diploma we earned, or our engagement and marriage. We're excited to share these precious moments. When words of saving grace take root in our hearts to change our lives for all eternity, we want to climb the highest hill in town and shout it out for all to hear. Indeed, our joy cannot be contained.

---

8. 2 Peter 3:18.
9. 1 Corinthians 13:1.
10. Romans 8:1.
11. Romans 2:15.
12. Galatians 5:13–14.

> *But if I say, "I will not mention his word or speak anymore in his name,"*
> *his word is in my heart like a fire, a fire shut up in my bones.*
> *I am weary of holding it in; indeed, I cannot.*
> (Jeremiah 20:9)

Freedom is the American dream. In fact, every oppressed human on Earth yearns to be liberated. Our Lord Jesus hears our groaning when we're repressed and He answers our heart's cry. Then, the Lord offers blessings upon blessings in an eternal freedom. The Good News Gospel is a covenant guarantee of this freedom. This kind of liberty needs a sure foundation and structure to make it strong and keep it strong. Jesus paid the price of our freedom on a cruel Roman cross on Mount Golgotha in an act of the greatest love. Because of Jesus' sacrificial death and resurrection, those who are in Christ and called by His name are set free from the curse of sin and death.

When we hear and receive the gift of saving grace, it's as if Jesus speaks for us the same words He spoke on Lazarus' behalf: "Take off the grave clothes and let him go."[13] By means of the abounding love Yeshua has shown to us, we can now love Him and delight in obeying Him. Jesus reveals Himself as the Rock—a sure foundation. The building blocks of this love-bought freedom are revealed in all of Jesus' teachings. He offered words of eternal life to us, and in these words of truth we are set free from the grave clothes that once bound us.

It's like every word Jesus spoke from the very beginning of time until today is a building stone of truth. His every word speaks life to all who will hear and sets us free to build our lives in Christ. It is for us to treasure His words and then live our lives in accord with His teaching. The path of freedom is sustainable for all eternity for those who endure in Jesus' teaching.

> *To the Jews who had believed him, Jesus said, "If you hold to my teaching, you are really my disciples. Then you will know the truth, and the truth will set you free."*
> (John 8:31–32)

Praise will flow from the mouths of those who delight in the law of the Lord. Meditating on God's decrees stirs us to exalt the Lord Almighty. Remembering the Lord's precepts puts a song in our hearts. Considering what the Almighty's hand has done inspires us to acclaim the Lord of all heaven and earth. When we partake of Christ, in whom the Law is fulfilled, we cannot be kept from lifting up holy hands in true worship and praise. The law of love written on our hearts makes us thirsty for wellsprings of the living water that perfectly satisfies. We will thirst no more. Those who hear God's councils

---

13. John 11:44.

are filled with a desire to be immersed, saturated in His words of wisdom and grace. Indeed, He satisfies us in a dry and thirsty land.

I remember the days of long ago; I meditate on all your works and consider what your hands have done. I spread out my hands to you; I thirst for you like a parched land.
(Psalm 143:5–6)

Verse 41 of Psalm 119 begins with the sixth letter of the Hebrew alphabet: ו "Waw" or "Vav." The prophet Ezra's purpose is to show his love for God's precepts, promises, laws, and commands. He builds verse by verse to show us the many facets of God's care, affection, and mercies revealed to us in God's law of love. Ezra shows us the effects of God's love in our everyday lives, in the words we speak, and in every interaction with our neighbors. There is great joy, strength, peace, and comfort in God's commands because they serve as a staff in the gentle hand of the Good Shepherd to guide and redirect our lives. The rod also serves as an instrument of wrath to defend us against those who would do us harm.

The psalmist shows us that every word of instruction is like a precious stone to build a sure and strong sanctuary of worship where we will sing out praises to our Lord God. The Lord's commands are like gates flung open to let us run free on the path of the Lord's precepts. His precious promises are like doors thrown open to welcome us into God's dwelling place.

Every stanza in Ezra's love song washes over us with affectionate choruses, delighted obedience, grace, mercy, compassion, and redemption. Yehovah's loving precepts set our hearts free and cause our mouths to overflow with praise for God who is above all gods, to our King who is above all kings, and to our Lord who is above all lords.

21. A Love Psalm
Q & A

1. What are the origins of the law of love that is written on our hearts?

2. How will you answer a neighbor who asks, "What makes you so hopeful all the time?"

3. Is it true that the words we speak reveal what is in our hearts?

4. Explain why ministries and service in spiritual gifts apart from love are little more than irritating noise.

5. Describe the fire that burns in our bones—the fire of God's love.

My Journal Notes:

Chapter 22
Love the Giver More Than the Gift

Key Scriptures:

- "Jesus replied, 'No one who puts a hand to the plow and looks back is fit for service in the kingdom of God.'" (Luke 9:62)

- "On that day no one who is on the housetop, with possessions inside, should go down to get them. Likewise, no one in the field should go back for anything. Remember Lot's wife!" (Luke 17:31–32)

- "Indeed, to them you are nothing more than one who sings love songs with a beautiful voice and plays an instrument well, for they hear your words but do not put them into practice." (Ezekiel 33:32)

The Lord of Hosts told Abraham to look up and count the stars to see the future He planned for his family. The people of Israel were instructed to observe the sun, moon, and stars Yehovah created. But, they were never to bow down to them.[1] Lot and his family were urged to leave the Jordan valley and flee to the hills, but not look back. In the same manner, the holy Scriptures call us to look up and cast life's cares and burdens upon the Lord. In this study, Jesus, Abraham, Lot, Elisha, and the people of Israel will help teach us why it is so important to hold our temporal blessings in an open hand and not allow our possessions own us. We'll learn why it's important to let go of material blessings when we are called to release them in Jesus name.

Jesus offered a parable to illustrate this truth. His story told of a man who was so short-sighted that he could only see that his barns were too small to hold all that he had gathered. This myopic man looked at the piles of goods God provided and decided it wasn't enough. If he lived in our day, the man might have said, "I want a bigger refrigerator. I want a larger garage. I want, I want, I want, and I want it now!" Rather than thankfulness and contentment in God's abundant blessings, he wanted to hoard even more. Loving these things too much didn't turn out very well for him.

But God said to him, "You fool! This very night your life will be demanded from you. Then who will get what you have prepared for yourself?"
This is how it will be with whoever stores up things for themselves but is not rich toward God.
(Luke 12:20–21)

---

[1]. Deuteronomy 4:19.

When Abraham and Lot separated their households and herds, Lot chose the lush green plains of the Jordan Valley over the sparse rolling hills of the Negev and then pitched his tents near Sodom. The bitter roots of depravity ran deep in Sodom and Gomorrah, and this violence caused Lot to grieve and call out to the Lord Almighty in anguish.

Our gracious and merciful Father in heaven always provides a way of escape for those who mourn over sin, especially their own. But too many can't escape the clutches of precious earthly possessions because they hold onto them too tight. We must never love life's blessings more than the Giver of all good gifts.

> *Flee for your lives! Don't look back, and don't stop anywhere in the plain!*
> *Flee to the mountains or you will be swept away!*
> (Genesis 19:17)

Elisha's calloused hands gripped the plow handles behind a yoke of oxen when Elijah found him. The ox team he worked with was a valuable tool to help him prepare the fields for spring. But then Elijah called him to be a plowman in heaven's domain, to prepare kingdom soil for the promised Seed of Israel. Without hesitation, Elisha bid his family farewell, sacrificed the oxen on an altar, and followed Elijah as his servant.

We too must be prepared to "sacrifice the oxen" and serve as bonded servants in the kingdom of heaven. But if we try to pack all our earthly possessions on our back, we will break our back and be unworthy to serve. We are called to be good stewards of the blessings God has given us, but we must hold them in an open hand. Indeed, they are not ours to possess, but to manage as godly overseers, and if need be, to give them up in order to serve. This is the heart of a love-driven servant.

> *He [Elisha] took his yoke of oxen and slaughtered them.*
> *He burned the plowing equipment to cook the meat and gave it to the people,*
> *and they ate. Then he set out to follow Elijah and became his servant.*
> (1 Kings 19:21)

Treasures we store up in heaven remain untarnished forever. They will not become moth-eaten or turn to rust, and the reason is simple: What we store up in heaven's storeroom is tested by fire or purified with water.[2] Things of temporal value are like wood, straw, and chaff that burn up in the fire and cannot be stored in heaven.

---

2. Numbers 31:23.

Every person born into the kingdom of heaven is called to serve toward strengthening the whole. Each one of us who is called by Jesus' holy name is given a job in the kingdom—an impossible work by means of our own strength. But this job is made possible as the Spirit of Christ anoints, gifts, and empowers God's people. The work we accomplish in the power and strength of the Holy Spirit is like precious gold that withstands the test of fire before it is stored up for us in the kingdom of heaven. We must not ever value the Spirit's good gifts more than the Giver of the gift because our work would then turn to straw, unable to be washed clean or pass the test of fire.

Do not store up for yourselves treasures on earth, where moths and vermin destroy, and where thieves break in and steal. But store up for yourselves treasures in heaven, where moths and vermin do not destroy, and where thieves do not break in and steal. For where your treasure is, there your heart will be also.
(Matthew 6:19–21)

Like a general leading jubilant troops returning victorious and laden with spoils, our Lord Jesus arose and conquered the grave. Our risen Yashua HaMachiach gives good gifts to all those who receive Him as their advocate. These spiritual gifts strengthen the body of Christ and make every part useful for the work of the Great Commission. All Jesus' followers who receive the gifts and make good use of them will see them grow, flourish and reveal the riches of Christ.

Enter into the fullness of Christ and receive the spiritual gifts that have been prepared for each one of us who are called by Jesus' name. All Jesus' disciples are included, whether to serve in an office of the church or to serve with other gifts that strengthen the church. We are called to gather together to minister and serve before our High Priest, Jesus Christ, who ascended to the right hand of the Father. We are called to serve as a functioning part of the body of Christ, inspired in love, and delighting to serve before our Lord and Savior. Let us love the Giver of good gifts above all else and serve humbly before our God.

When he ascended on high, he took many captives and gave gifts to his people.
(Ephesians 4:8)

The Great I AM turned the heart of King Cyrus to help Israel's exiles return to Jerusalem so they could build a temple to worship the Lord God. With seventy years of exile in a foreign land completed as prophesied by Jeremiah, the Lord gave His people favor before the king so they could go in peace to their homeland. Each person who returned to Israel did so with a purpose—to serve in the rebuilding of Jerusalem and build the temple to

God's holy name. They brought with them treasures of silver, gold, household goods, and their herds of sheep and cattle acquired in a foreign land. But the family possessions were not held as their own.

Because of their love for Yehovah God and His place of worship, they offered their valuables for construction of the temple where they would worship and serve before the Lord. Rather than store up goods in barns, they stored up treasure in the kingdom of heaven. This same loving generosity manifested itself again in the newly baptized converts as the early church began, as recorded in the book of Acts.[3]

*Then the family heads of Judah and Benjamin, and the priests and Levites–everyone whose heart God had moved–prepared to go up and build the house of the L*ORD *in Jerusalem. All their neighbors assisted them with articles of silver and gold, with goods and livestock, and with valuable gifts, in addition to all the freewill offerings.*
(Ezra 1:5–6)

Gifts are often re-gifted when they're not useful to us. But spiritual gifts, given as the Spirit wills, are a great treasure worth keeping. Their value increases as we give of ourselves to serve others in accord with our gift. The beauty of this is that the gift is strengthened in us when we give in service to our neighbors. It's like pouring water from our cup for someone who is thirsty, only to find that our cup is full to the brim and still overflowing. This is the miraculous beauty of spiritual gifts. When we give from the gift empowered in us, the recipient is strengthened and the giver's spiritual gift is enhanced. Even more, when it is given in love, the bond of Christ's love is strengthened.

When we see this truth at work in our lives, our love for the Giver of the gifts will grow, our affections for those to whom we minister will flourish, and our joy in serving will increase. The greatest of all gifts from the Spirit of Christ is the gift of love. Christ's love keeps us from loving the gift more than the Giver of the gift, and because of this, the gift of love will be like the harmony of well-orchestrated music. Without it, all spiritual gifts are little more than noise.[4]

Each of you should use whatever gift you have received to serve others, as faithful stewards of God's grace in its various forms.
(1 Peter 4:10)

---

3. Acts 4:32–37.
4. 1 Corinthians 13:1.

THE GREATEST LOVE

Years ago, I met a gentleman and his wife who had fled Germany and made their way across the Mediterranean Sea to their ancestral homeland in Israel. Before their ship could dock at Haifa, the British closed the nation to immigrants. Asaf and Hania[5] decided to jump over the side of the transport ship and swim to shore, where the underground Zionist militia took them in. The stories he told about the dilemmas many families faced who were left behind in Germany made their predicament clear. Jewish family members had built very successful careers and businesses in Germany. They owned banks, jewelry stores, theaters, and they were among the best doctors and scientists. How could they leave everything behind?

The nation of Israel was open so they could return to their homeland to build a new life and start over again in a land their ancestors inhabited. But many of them refused because their roots were too deep in Europe's soil. Yehovah God opened the doors wide for them to return to Israel, but they wouldn't go. The Lord knew what evil days lay ahead in the near future and He gave them a way of escape, but they couldn't leave because their success and possessions weighed them down. Like every parent on Earth, they wanted to provide security for their loved ones and hesitated to give up the stability of careers and family. .

Even when our hand is on the plow behind a yoke of prized oxen, we should be ready to let go of Earth's good blessings. If we don't, these possessions will turn our heads to look back rather than forward. For those who refuse to let go, their barns and storage sheds will never be big enough. We must sacrifice the oxen in order to press on and go forward. When called to do so, we must unload our possessions to serve the cause of the kingdom of heaven. It's like that 40-pound backpack we throw off before we make a final ascent to the top of the mountain. Whether we are called to serve while also being good stewards of many good things, or called to sell all and serve, we must not get too attached to our temporal things and allow them to own us or hold us back. What do you choose to love?

---

5. Names changed to protect the privacy of those involved.

22. Love the Giver More Than the Gift
Q & A

1. How is it possible for our material possessions to own us?

2. What is the lesson we learn from Elisha as he sacrifices his team of oxen when called to serve Elijah?

3. What is the danger of loving the gift more than the Giver of the gift?

4. Describe the power and effect as we pour out of our cup to someone who is thirsty.

My Journal Notes:

Chapter 23
The Greatest Love Song

Key Scriptures:

- "I will sing for the one I love a song about his vineyard: My loved one had a vineyard on a fertile hillside." (Isaiah 5:1)
- "Sing about a fruitful vineyard: I, the LORD, watch over it; I water it continually. I guard it day and night so that no one may harm it." (Isaiah 27:2–3)

In this study, Moses' prophetic song in Deuteronomy 32 will instruct us so we may know God's immeasurable love. His song proclaims the Great I AM's loving care and protection. His inspired verses teach us the loving nature of the Father's correction and discipline. In every word he voices, we can see Messiah who pressed on toward the cross in a show of the greatest love ever known in all heaven and earth.

1st Sonnet

When God's word first enlightens us, our eyes will open to see our sin, our sinfulness, and our need of Christ's redemptive work. When we hear the glory of God declared, it causes us to yearn for Jesus, the resurrected Messiah. When we repent, come to saving faith, and are baptized, the love of Christ blossoms and bears fruit in us. By faith, the law of love is written on our hearts. This love sprouts and flourishes by means of a saving faith in Jesus our Lord and Savior.

As new creations in Christ, we become hungry for the teaching of God's word. This instruction is like fresh rain to water the seed of faith planted in our hearts. God's promises are like morning dew on budding leaves. God's justice, as revealed in the holy Scriptures, inspires us and compels us to lift up holy hands to exalt the Lord Almighty for the greatness of His bountiful love toward all humankind.

Listen, you heavens, and I will speak; hear, you earth, the words of my mouth. Let my teaching fall like rain and my words descend like dew, like showers on new grass, like abundant rain on tender plants. I will proclaim the name of the LORD. Oh, praise the greatness of our God! He is the Rock, his works are perfect, and all his ways are just. A faithful God who does no wrong, upright and just is he.
(Deuteronomy 32:1–4)

2nd **Sonnet**

O Lord, break our hearts because of our sin and depravity. Cause our hearts to repent before the throne of grace. Indeed, our corruption has robbed us of the unifying power of our faith. Distracted spiritual love causes us to scorn gathering in Jesus' name. The deviant nature of our culture's sexuality has deprived Christians of intimate fellowship with our Heavenly Father. The kind of love we have created on our own is like parasitic mistletoe that leaches moisture and nutrients from the host tree. Christmas celebrants use a sprig of mistletoe to invite kisses in celebration of the season, but the leaves that once grew to mimic the host tree are, in reality, destructive and parasitic. Too many churches today are laden with parasitic growth and branches of the tree are dying.

We have redefined love to mean gratification of self, and in this way we have polluted a gift offered as pure, righteous, and unblemished affection. Sexual sins in the church violate too many people, destroy their faith, crush their souls, and drive them from fellowship. This pervasive violence has scattered the sheep and made them vulnerable to the enemies of Christ.

All sins of a sexual nature are most destructive because they are like a cancer that devours spirit, soul, and body. Sexual sin is a violation of and insult to the loving, intimate relationship that God desires with us. Illicit intimacies are an idolatry of self—idolizing what pleases our eyes. Sensual sins pollute our spirit's connection to the Holy Spirit and join it to the darkness of death and the judgment of the unrighteous.

God desires sweet, loving, tender, and intimate communion with us, but we have given ourselves to another. "Therefore God gave them over in the sinful desires of their hearts to sexual impurity for the degrading of their bodies with one another. They exchanged the truth about God for a lie, and worshiped and served created things rather than the Creator—who is forever praised. Amen."[1]

Come with me to the throne of grace. Let us confess our sin and sinfulness so that we may receive the forgiveness, grace, and mercy of our Lord and Savior.

> *They are corrupt and not his children; to their shame they are a warped and crooked generation. Is this the way you repay the L*ORD*, you foolish and unwise people?*
> *Is he not your Father, your Creator, who made you and formed you?*
> *Remember the days of old; consider the generations long past.*
> *Ask your father and he will tell you, your elders, and they will explain to you.*
> (Deuteronomy 32:5–7)

---

1. Romans 1:24–25.

3rd **Sonnet**

With abundant love and compassion, the Lord Almighty has adorned His people like a bride in all her decorum. He wraps us in His robes of righteousness.[2] We are clothed, as if with the finest embroidered linen, and bejeweled with ornaments of silver, gold, and precious stones.[3] Our heavenly Father has set our boundaries in pleasant places. God provides us the finest food, the best of the land to make us grow healthy and strong in body, soul, and spirit. The King who is above all kings welcomes us to be seated with Him to reflect His glory for all to see.[4] Because of His abundant love, He holds us in the hollow of His hands, leads us to dwell us in the shelter of the Most High, and gives us rest in the shadow of the Almighty.[5] By the power of the Word and the Spirit of Christ, the Bridegroom has adorned us with heaven's beauty. All this is an expression of his immeasurable love for us.

When the Most High gave the nations their inheritance, when he divided all mankind,
he set up boundaries for the peoples according to the number of the sons of Israel.
For the LORD's portion is his people, Jacob his allotted inheritance.

In a desert land he found him, in a barren and howling waste.

He shielded him and cared for him; he guarded him as the apple of his eye,

like an eagle that stirs up its nest and hovers over its young,
that spreads its wings to catch them and carries them aloft.
The LORD alone led him; no foreign god was with him.

He made him ride on the heights of the land and fed him with the fruit of the fields.
He nourished him with honey from the rock, and with oil from the flinty crag,
with curds and milk from herd and flock and with fattened lambs and goats,
with choice rams of Bashan and the finest kernels of wheat.

You drank the foaming blood of the grape.

(Deuteronomy 32:8–14)

---

2. Isaiah 61:10.
3. Ezekiel 16:9–14.
4. Ephesians 2:6–7.
5. Psalm 91:1.

4th **Sonnet**

Too many Christians attempt to recreate a Jesus to their own liking and form a god in their own image. Then, the Sunday morning assembly becomes a celebration of what their own hands have made.[6] We are like Peter who tried to redirect Jesus from His mission. He rebuked Jesus, saying, "Never, Lord! This shall never happen to you."[7] When we create our own Jesus to serve our own purpose and then call our god by the same name as the only Son of God, this violates the commandment to not "take the Lord's name in vain"[8] in the vilest way possible.

A self-serving way of thinking, when left unchecked, leads us to worship the work of our own hands, a god of our own making. The heavenly Father's abundant love and bountiful provision will never be enough. The appetite of a false god is never satisfied. Those who worship in this way need to hear Jesus' response: "Get behind me, Satan! You are a stumbling block to me; you do not have in mind the concerns of God, but merely human concerns."[9]

Americans have enjoyed the fat of the land and the blessings of prosperity for so long that we think we deserve it. We're quite sure we have earned this bounty on our own, and it's ours to keep. We were once grafted into the True Vine, Jesus Christ, but we have broken ourselves off to be grafted into the vine of iniquity that is fed by a root of bitterness.[10] We once sowed the seed of the Word of God in fallow ground, but now we sow wild seed and reap a harvest of chaos. There was a time when we ministered and served by means of God's holy fire, the fire of the Spirit of Christ, but now we play with a fire of our own making.[11]

With each wild seed we sow, we store up sorrows that will eventually overwhelm us. It's like our life's vessel gets filled to the bursting point and one more illicit act will cause it to burst with the consequences.

The brutal reality is that the idolatry of self is self-destructive. And yet, the Lord Almighty, in His abundant love and mercy, will come against this sin before its darkness destroys us. He is quick to forgive and clean away our sinfulness. But if we again and again refuse to repent and receive Christ's grace and mercy, there is nothing left but to release us to the full bent of our wicked ways.

---

6. Acts 7:41.
7. Mathew 16:22.
8. Exodus 20:7.
9. Matthew 16:23.
10. Hebrews 12:15.
11. Leviticus 10:1.

Jeshurun grew fat and kicked; filled with food, they became heavy and sleek. They abandoned the God who made them and rejected the Rock their Savior. They made him jealous with their foreign gods and angered him with their detestable idols. They sacrificed to false gods, which are not God—gods they had not known, gods that recently appeared, gods your ancestors did not fear. You deserted the Rock, who fathered you; you forgot the God who gave you birth.

The Lord saw this and rejected them because he was angered by his sons and daughters. "I will hide my face from them," he said, "and see what their end will be; for they are a perverse generation, children who are unfaithful. They made me jealous by what is no god and angered me with their worthless idols. I will make them envious by those who are not a people; I will make them angry by a nation that has no understanding. For a fire will be kindled by my wrath, one that burns down to the realm of the dead below. It will devour the earth and its harvests and set afire the foundations of the mountains.

"I will heap calamities on them and spend my arrows against them. I will send wasting famine against them, consuming pestilence and deadly plague; I will send against them the fangs of wild beasts, the venom of vipers that glide in the dust. In the street the sword will make them childless; in their homes terror will reign. The young men and young women will perish, the infants and those with gray hair. I said I would scatter them and erase their name from human memory, but I dreaded the taunt of the enemy, lest the adversary misunderstand and say, 'Our hand has triumphed; the Lord has not done all this.'"

They are a nation without sense, there is no discernment in them. If only they were wise and would understand this and discern what their end will be! How could one man chase a thousand, or two put ten thousand to flight, unless their Rock had sold them, unless the Lord had given them up? For their rock is not like our Rock, as even our enemies concede. Their vine comes from the vine of Sodom and from the fields of Gomorrah. Their grapes are filled with poison, and their clusters with bitterness. Their wine is the venom of serpents, the deadly poison of cobras.

"Have I not kept this in reserve and sealed it in my vaults? It is mine to avenge; I will repay. In due time their foot will slip; their day of disaster is near and their doom rushes upon them."

(Deuteronomy 32:15–35)

5th **Sonnet**

From the first words of creation to the final words of Revelation, the Scriptures reveal a clear path of atonement for sin. In the first words of the Genesis account of creation, our Redeemer is revealed as the Word of creation. But Satan snaked his way with a venomous hiss to tempt Eve and Adam and capture them in the clutches of death. Then Elohim who walked with Adam and Eve in the garden, in abundant grace and mercy, showed compassion and forgiveness and provided a covering for their nakedness.

Their sin was covered, but they lost their garden paradise.

Then people multiplied and spread throughout the land and the darkness of sin flourished among them. In His faithfulness, the Lord raised up a prophet in Noah, a preacher of righteousness[12] to build a seaworthy ship as a warning against their depravity. The ark served as an illustrated sermon to warn them of the wrath to come. This vessel offered a picture of God's saving grace as He gathered Noah's family and brought the animals of the Earth two by two. Then God closed the door and sealed them all inside, safe from the wrath poured out to destroy the sin that ravaged the whole Earth.

The history of the tribes of Israel is one of a constant rising and falling. The people were brought out of slavery in Egypt. They sang a great song of deliverance, and then turned around to grumble in their tents against their Deliverer. While Moses remained on the mountain to receive God's Law, they made a golden idol in the image of a calf. There were severe consequences for their waywardness. But then, again, God's mercies triumphed over judgment. The Lord of Hosts held out His hands of mercy and forgiveness to a wayward people. God was faithful to His promises even when they were not, and He brought them into His bountiful promised land. They harvested what they didn't plant. They lived in houses they didn't build.

Then the people who were called by the Lord's holy name brought shame upon His name by their idolatry yet again. They offered their newborn babies as offerings to heinous false gods. They embraced the idols of neighboring nations. God showed His abundant love and mercy by raising up prophets to warn them of their sin and call them to repentance. But they stopped up their ears, threw God's messengers out, and killed the prophets. As a result, the Lord raised up a foreign conqueror to break them in their wickedness. He removed them from the land of promise and made them exiles in a foreign land.

Finally, in every instance, God brought the people to repent of their sin. And then, with a mighty hand and outstretched arm, rescued His people

---

12. 2 Peter 2:5.

from the scepter of wicked rulers.[13] The cruelest of these rulers were the chains of their own sin. But again and again, God showed His long-suffering love for His people. His love-driven mercies were poured out afresh, and He brought His people back to the Promised Land where they could worship the Lord their God in all holiness.

We are not unlike the tribes of Israel. We have failed to love with our whole hearts and we're complacent in our sin. We have not loved the Lord God with our whole mind and spirit.[14] Our hearts are not grieved because of our own sin and offenses against the Creator of all heaven and earth. The Earth is ravaged because of the sins of its inhabitants. We have brought shame upon God's holy name. Must we be shaken to the core before we will repent of our sinful attitude and mindset? We have exploited the Lord's beautiful gifts and attempted to possess them as our own. But God's holy word, by the power of the Holy Spirit, exposes our sin. The law of love written on our hearts shows us our need of Christ's forgiveness and mercy. With broken hearts, we are brought to repentance for the darkness of sin and the destruction it brought about upon our families and neighbors. If we refuse to repent and receive God's abundant grace, we are left to the gods of our own making.

The LORD will vindicate his people and relent concerning his servants when he sees their strength is gone and no one is left, slave or free. He will say: "Now where are their gods, the rock they took refuge in, the gods who ate the fat of their sacrifices and drank the wine of their drink offerings? Let them rise up to help you! Let them give you shelter!
(Deuteronomy 32:36–38)

6th Sonnet

Throughout history, God's people have faced many enemies. But we don't enter the struggle on our own. Indeed, the fight has never been ours alone. The battle is the Lord's.[15] Too often, we are offended when we hear the Lord's prophet proclaim, "I will take vengeance on my adversaries." Are the words consistent with God who shows us immeasurable love—the greatest love? When we finally realize that these harsh words are meant for God's enemies who caused harm to His people, we begin to understand the full extent of His abundant love. If the Lord of Hosts did not rise up in vengeance and throw down those who are determined to destroy His sons and daughters, His love would be incomplete.

Even when our enemy is the sinful attitude in our own heart, our Father will cleanse us of this defiance and then heal our wounded heart. By the pow-

---
13. Psalm 125:3.
14. Mathew 22:37.
15. 2 Chronicles 20:15.

er of the Word and the Holy Spirit, Abba Father shows His loving kindness to lead our hearts to repentance and then restore us to sweet fellowship. Once again, we will lift up holy hands to worship in spirit and in truth. Our worship will be spiritual and real.

God of the armies of heaven wields His sharpened sword to lay His enemies low. Those who come under the Lord's righteous judgments are cut down so they can no longer do harm to the sheep of His pasture. The Lord spoke of this love through the prophet Zechariah: "For he who touches you touches the apple of his eye."[16] Our heavenly Father protects us, cherishes us, carefully watches over us, and covers us in the shadow of His wings. All those who would do us harm, take warning, for Yahweh is a jealous God who will not allow us to be dragged away. The prowling lion cannot snatch lambs from the Shepherd's flock.

See now that I myself am he! There is no god besides me. I put to death and I bring to life, I have wounded and I will heal, and no one can deliver out of my hand.

I lift my hand to heaven and solemnly swear: As surely as I live forever, when I sharpen my flashing sword and my hand grasps it in judgment, I will take vengeance on my adversaries and repay those who hate me.

I will make my arrows drunk with blood, while my sword devours flesh: the blood of the slain and the captives, the heads of the enemy leaders.

(Deuteronomy 32:39–42)

Our Prayer: Lord Jesus, hold us so close that we can hear your heartbeat, the vibrant pulse that flows with love, righteousness, justice, forgiveness, mercy, and saving grace. O Lord make our hearts beat with this same rhythm. Lord, have mercy on us for we are sinners. Cleanse us of all unrighteousness, wash us, and make us clean. Make our mouths proclaim the joy of your saving grace to all who will hear, for we have been set free from the clutches of sin, Satan, and death—all because of the greatest love ever known.

7th Sonnet

We serve an awesome God who writes our names in the Book of Life. The Creator of all heaven and earth chooses those whom He will so we may be called by His holy name. He calls us out of the world's darkness into the Light of Christ. By the power of His word and conviction of the Holy Spirit, He leads us to grieve over our sin and repent. Jesus, the Lamb of God, made atonement for our

---

16. Zechariah 2:8.

sins and died in our place so that by the blood of the Lamb we may be washed clean—whiter than freshly fallen snow.[17] In the waters of holy baptism, we are made new creations in Christ and made to be one in His body, the Church.

By means of the power of resurrection, we are raised up and set free from the power of sin, Satan, and death. Jesus won a mighty victory and death lost its sting.[18] No longer is death master over us.[19] Now we can stand as victors with Christ and rejoice in the God of our Salvation. The Lord our Redeemer loved us first,[20] and so He is our first love. The law of love is now written on our hearts and compels us to worship, serve, and minister in Jesus' name. With the heart of a servant, we step out every day of our lives with purpose so we may walk in delighted obedience.[21]

God's immeasurable love powerfully changes our lives. We grieve when our actions come into conflict with the law of love because His love floods our hearts. Then we will run to Jesus for forgiveness and mercy, and we will be cleansed from even the stain of our sin. We are set free because the penalty of sin has been paid on our behalf.[22]

Rejoice, you nations, with his people, for he will avenge the blood of his servants; he will take vengeance on his enemies and make atonement for his land and people.
(Deuteronomy 32:43)

The Finale

Moses sang out with a faith-inspired prophetic song so the people could hear his words and take them to heart. Then, what filled their hearts overflowed in love-inspired words that continue to effect faith in their children and grandchildren. The words of Moses' song were offered as affectionate warnings and encouragements, as life to God's people. By means of an Abraham-like faith, the words led them to saving grace and eternal life.[23]

Moses' song is a beautiful revelation of the nature of God's love for all those who are called by His holy name. For the people who might only find his singing entertaining, Moses emphasized that these were not frivolous words. These inspired oracles were meant to permeate every part of their lives. Their everyday words, actions, and the work of their hands must be reflections of God's multifaceted and abundant love manifested in the sheep of His pasture.

17. Psalm 51:7.
18. 1 Corinthians 15:55.
19. Romans 6:9.
20. 1 John 4:19.
21. John 14:15.
22. Romans 6:23.
23. John 5:39.

The love Moses prophesied didn't originate in the imagination of a composer for a movie's musical score. Israel's prophet didn't promote a fantasy-romance kind of love. Nor is his song a one-sided, "only what we desire" kind of love. Heaven's love is not limited by human passions. God's love is so vast, multi-faceted, and all-encompassing that when we cross over the great divide into His eternal Promised Land, it may take us an eternity to grasp the richness of the greatest love ever known.

Moses came with Joshua son of Nun and spoke all the words of this song in the hearing of the people. When Moses finished reciting all these words to all Israel, he said to them, "Take to heart all the words I have solemnly declared to you this day, so that you may command your children to obey carefully all the words of this law. They are not just idle words for you–they are your life. By them you will live long in the land you are crossing the Jordan to possess."
(Deuteronomy 32:44–47)

After Moses led the people of Israel out of bondage in Egypt, he sang out with triumphant, prophetic words to celebrate the Lord's mighty victory. Israel's deliverer prefigures our Deliverer, Jesus Christ, who frees us from the oppression of sin, Satan, and death. When Christ Jesus comes into His final victory, we will sing out with a new song in celebration of our Redeemer, because "of the greatness of his government and peace there will be no end." He will have established and will uphold His rule with justice and righteousness forever.[24] The words of the tunes that once bound us in darkness will go up in smoke and be blown away in the wind of the Spirit. Now we are free to join with our Lord Jesus and the holy angels to sing a victorious new song. The words of this love song will ring out for all eternity.

And they sang a new song, saying:

"You are worthy to take the scroll and to open its seals, because you were slain, and with your blood you purchased for God persons from every tribe and language and people and nation. You have made them to be a kingdom and priests to serve our God, and they will reign on the earth."

(Revelation 5:9–10)

---

24. Isaiah 9:7.

23. The Greatest Love Song
Q & A

1. What is the significance of the adornments given to beautify the bride of Christ?

2. How do people create a Jesus of their own design and what is the danger of doing so?

3. What is the effect of the Father's unchanging, faithful love on all those who are called by His holy name?

4. Describe your sense of freedom that comes from giving up the lyrics of popular love songs, and then singing Jesus' new song in harmony with heaven's angels.

5. Why is the sword of the Lord an important instrument of love for all the sheep of His pasture?

My Journal Notes:

Chapter 24
Love is Knocking at Your Heart's Door

Key Scriptures:

- "Behold, I stand at the door and knock. If anyone hears my voice and opens the door, I will come in to him and eat with him, and he with me." (Revelation 3:20 ESV)

- "Come, all you who are thirsty, come to the waters; and you who have no money, come, buy and eat! Come, buy wine and milk without money and without cost." (Isaiah 55:1)

This is a decisive step as we reach the summit of this study and come to see love's eternal purpose. Indeed, today is the day to enter into the joy of Salvation held out to us in Jesus' nail scarred hands. God's words and commands show us our sin and our need for Christ Jesus and His abundant love. The Gospel message is presented here as an invitation to receive His saving grace for forgiveness and cleansing of sin. The book of Romans opens the door to the Gospel message, revealing these life-giving words to enlighten and lead us to saving faith. This is the Gospel's path that beckons us with words to serve as milestones of faith that lead to Christ. The book of Romans offers a clear path to saving grace, emphasizing Jesus' life-giving words that testified He is the Way, the Truth, and the Life, and there is no other way. In Paul's letter to the Ephesians, he reinforces these crucial Gospel truths found in Romans.

This study will lead us to know that, as we stand before the Lord, there is no difference between men and women. The color of our skin isn't an issue, and there is no special advantage even for descendants of the tribe of Judah.[1] We'll learn that we have no righteousness of our own, but we're not without hope because our Lord Jesus will cover us with His robe of righteousness. Though we are undeserving, we are wrapped in Jesus' righteousness so that we may come before the throne of Grace with all boldness to stand in God's favor.

We'll learn that our fallen nature is traced back to Adam's original sin. This study will teach us that faith to believe Jesus is the Christ, Son of the Living God, is only possible because of His abundant love for us. This is the love that compelled Him to give His body to be broken and His blood to be shed to redeem us from the chains of our sin.

---

1. Acts 10:34–35.

> *This righteousness is given through faith in Jesus Christ to all who believe. There is no difference between Jew and Gentile, for all have sinned and fall short of the glory of God, and all are justified freely by his grace through the redemption that came by Christ Jesus.*
> (Romans 3:22–24)

It doesn't seem fair at first that sin and corruption entered the world because one man broke his covenant with God and sinned against the Lord. Consider the nature of slavery to help understand this reality. Adam's original sin sold all of his progeny into clutches of sin and death. This is like the days when the cruelty of slavery was legal. A child born to a slave automatically became enslaved from birth. Sin entered the world by Adam, and all who come after Adam are therefore born in bondage to sin. Because of Adam's sin, we are born with stains that make us sinners like our ancestor. We are born in need of redemption. Our lives unfold as fallible mortals. But when we see the righteousness of Jesus Christ and the wonders of the Lord Almighty, we will realize our need of Christ and His forgiveness and mercy.

> *Therefore, just as sin entered the world through one man, and death through sin, and in this way death came to all people, because all sinned.*
> (Romans 5:12)

We have all been born as slaves to sin and the penalty for sin is death. But our Lord Jesus broke the curse by dying in our place for our sin, and the sin of the world. In Christ, we are set free from sin, Satan, and death. Is there anything better than to become a bondservant of the Most High God who redeemed our life? The path Christians plod on this Earth seems like an uphill battle. It's like a road through a dry and thirsty land that is rocky and narrow, unlike the wide and smooth downhill slope that leads to death. But we have an eternal hope and an ever-present help in Jesus Christ our Lord. Our Yeshua is joy, strength, peace, and comfort. He dwells in us and we abide in Him. Our Redeemer takes hold of us by our right hand and says to us, "Do not be afraid."[2] As faith is planted in our heart of hearts it springs up to make us a new creation in Christ. When we're made a brand-new person, it's a good time to stand up and shout, "Hallelu yah!"[3] Indeed, we have been set free in Christ.

> *But now that you have been set free from sin and have become slaves of God, the benefit you reap leads to holiness, and the result is eternal life. For the wages of sin is death, but the gift of God is eternal life in Christ Jesus our Lord.*
> (Romans 6:22–23)

---

2. Isaiah 41:13–14.
3. Psalm 148:1.

Divine revelation is the means of revealing Jesus the Christ as Lord and Savior, Redeemer of our lost soul, and as the resurrected Messiah. When our eyes are opened to see how vast the love of God is for us, when we see God in all His glory, we will be horrified at our sinful condition. Our own muck and depravity, in contrast with God's holiness, will cause us even more alarm. We are brought to Jesus in our dark and dingy condition to see the brightness and majesty of the Lord God, and this will cause us to be shaken to the core of our being.

In our moment of shock, when we see our guilt and obnoxious state and realize that we are a hopeless case, our Lord Jesus opens our eyes to see that, even while we were caught in our sin, He paid the penalty to free us from those chains.

> *But God demonstrates his own love for us in this:*
> *While we were still sinners, Christ died for us.*
> (Romans 5:8)

Jesus is the narrow way, the door, the gate for us to enter into the Father's eternal rest. Jesus is Immanuel, born as a man, who walked among us. He taught, healed, and called the dead back to life. Jesus, the Lamb of God, gave His blood to be shed and, by His own shed blood, entered into the holy place to serve as High Priest before God's people. We are blood-bought sons and daughters whom He ushers before the Father as the redeemed, cleansed and wrapped in His righteousness. We cannot come to our heavenly Father in any other way than to believe and receive God's one and only son as Lord and Savior.

> *Jesus answered, "I am the way and the truth and the life.*
> *No one comes to the Father except through me."*
> (John 14:6)

Whatever fills our heart will inevitably come out as the words we speak.[4] Pious words can't save us, but the faith God plants in our hearts will cause us to confess with a confident, unshakable declaration of Jesus as our resurrected Christ, our Messiah. This is not an intellectual assent, the result of proofs for the veracity of Bible history. We can agree that Jesus was born and placed in a real manger, and that wise men came from the East to worship baby Jesus in Bethlehem, but agreement with historical proofs does not sow the seeds of saving faith in our hearts. Accepting historical evidence that a man named Pilot really existed and gave the order for Jesus to be crucified is not the means of salvation. We come to believe when a miraculous faith is seeded in our hearts as we hear the word of God. By this faith, we come to believe in

---

4. Luke 6:45.

Christ Jesus as Lord, and are granted right standing before the Father. With this assurance in our hearts, we are compelled to profess our faith. Indeed, if we don't tell someone about what God has done for us, the fire will burn in our hearts until we can no longer keep it in.[5]

> *If you declare with your mouth, "Jesus is Lord," and believe in your heart that God raised him from the dead, you will be saved. For it is with your heart that you believe and are justified, and it is with your mouth that you profess your faith and are saved.*
> (Romans 10:9–10)

Before time began, God knew our names. All who were appointed to eternal life were written down in the Lamb's book of life.[6] In addition, the Lord prepared a job for each one of His children to accomplish during their time on Earth.[7] The country we live in, the hospital where we were born, and the town where we grew up didn't even exist when God made note of His plan for our lives. Indeed, He created us to do good work to advance the kingdom of heaven.

An abundance of God's grace is poured out on those who come to saving faith. The Lord's bounty is with good purpose. By faith we have been redeemed—not because of our special natural gifts and talents or the great things we can do, but because we are chosen, set apart to receive Jesus' gift of saving faith.

For all those for whom Yehovah God prepared a great work, there is no cause for boasting. For we who have a humble work to accomplish in our lifetime, there is no need to brag. Whether great or humble, our work is an unearned gift of an impossible mission that is beyond our strength and ability. When we accomplish our work by the anointing, gifting, and empowering work of the Holy Spirit, this is evidence of the redemptive power of Christ at work in us.

> *For it is by grace you have been saved, through faith–and this is not from yourselves, it is the gift of God–not by works, so that no one can boast.*
> *For we are God's handiwork, created in Christ Jesus to do good works, which God prepared in advance for us to do.*
> (Ephesians 2:8–10)

The word "all" is used in the following verses twice, and backed up with an "everyone." This emphasis is purposed to reveal God's heart toward each and every one who calls on the name of the Lord. The Lord God is gracious and merciful, overflowing with goodness, and gives favor to people of every

---

5. Jeremiah 20:9.
6. Revelation 21:27.
7. Ephesians 2:10.

race and nation. But, in fact, no one seeks Him[8] until we hear and receive the Good News of His saving grace. When we hear the redemptive words of the holy Scriptures, our hearts compel us to call on the Lord for salvation. Paul's inspired words are a written guarantee that the Lord God will always hear our call and will always answer:

> *The same Lord is Lord of all and richly blesses all who call on him, for,*
> *"Everyone who calls on the name of the Lord will be saved."*
> (Romans 10:12–13)

Everyone is called to come to the throne of grace. Jesus suffered and died on behalf of all people who live on earth. Because of this, there is no one who has ever walked on this earth who has not been called. But few will hear God's call with ears of faith.[9] God's faithful witnesses in the sky—the sun, moon, and stars—declare God's glory.[10] But who has believed and obeyed the Gospel's call? When God's word is proclaimed in our hearing, the Word comes to life in our heart, soul, and spirit. Seeds of faith are planted in us to believe and receive the Gospel message. Many will hear and reject His message as foolishness. In rebelliousness, the Word will harden their hearts to the Good News. But to the redeemed, the Word is the power of God.[11]

For those who gladly receive the message and are made new creations in Christ, let our feet be spurred with Gospel truth so we may proclaim the Good News in every corner of the world for all to hear. Let's joyfully answer Jesus' command of the Great Commission to: "Go and make disciples of all nations, baptizing them in the name of the Father and of the Son and of the Holy Spirit, and teaching them to obey everything I have commanded you. And surely I am with you always, to the very end of the age."[12]

> *But they have not all obeyed the gospel. For Isaiah says, "Lord, who has believed what he*
> *has heard from us?" So faith comes from hearing, and hearing through the word of Christ.*
> *But I ask, have they not heard? Indeed they have, for*
> *"Their voice has gone out to all the earth, and their words to the ends of the world."*
> (Romans 10:16–18 ESV)

The Apostle Paul served as a devoted messenger to pass on the faith given to him. His epistles still speak life-giving words of saving faith to all who will hear. What have we believed because of Paul's testimony? We believe that Jesus, God's only Son, was born in the flesh and walked among us as Imman-

---

8. Romans 3:11.
9. Matthew 22:14.
10. Psalm 19:1.
11. 1 Corinthians 1:18.
12. Matthew 28:19–20.

uel, God with us. We believe the witnesses in the Bible that tell us Jesus died in our place, for our sin, descended into hell to seal His victory, and then rose from the dead. This is the essence of our Christian faith. By means of faith, we can live in expectation because our Lord Jesus Christ promised to prepare a place for us to spend eternity with Him, and will soon return to take us home. This is what we believe and we can rest assured in this faith.

> *For what I received I passed on to you as of first importance:*
> *that Christ died for our sins according to the Scriptures, that he was buried,*
> *that he was raised on the third day according to the Scriptures.*
> *(1 Corinthians 15:3–4)*

The power and effect of God's word is to wake up our ears to hear life-giving words of the Gospel that call us to Christ. It's the best Good News ever when we hear Jesus beckon to us, "I am the way and the truth and the life. No one comes to the Father except through me."[13] We have violated God's commands and know that we are sinners, and because of this our hearts break out in a repentant plea. There is no doubt in our heart and mind that, apart from Christ who died in our place and for our sin, we have no hope of right standing before Father God. In the light of Christ, and by the Word who existed from the beginning, we can finally see that Jesus is the Christ, Son of the living God, begotten of the Father before the world began, born of the virgin Mary, and He has redeemed us by His shed blood. The last Adam, Jesus Christ, purchased our redemption and saved us from the penalties of the first Adam's fall. These words are the seeds of faith that are sown in our heart of hearts so that we may believe and receive forgiveness and mercy, the gift of life, and the promise that we will live forever with our heavenly Father.

When our Lord Jesus calls us to be one with Him in His suffering, death, and resurrection, these words sound like the sweetest, most merciful, and life-giving sounds our ears will ever hear. Our hearts are crushed at hearing of His suffering and dying on our behalf, for our sin, in our place. And our hearts rejoice to cross the threshold as the bride of Christ, to live as He lived, to walk as He walked, to serve as He served, and to proclaim the Gospel that has saved us from the power of sin, Satan, and death.

The Apostle Paul provided us the essential message of the Gospel in a nutshell:

Christ died for our sins as foreshadowed in the Law and foretold by the prophets.

Jesus died on the cross and was buried.

---

13. John 14:6.

Jesus was raised on the third day, just as the Scriptures prophesied.

The resurrected Christ appeared to Peter, the Twelve disciples, and many others. [14]

Jesus holds out nail-scarred hands to each one of us, saying, "Come to me all who are poor, broken hearted, bruised, humiliated, wounded, torn, ensnared in the chains of sin, prisoners, weary, or overloaded with life's cares. All who are bound up in despair; come one and all and I will give you rest."[15] Our ears are filled with words of His glory and majesty. Our hearts rejoice to hear of His loving kindness and mercies. And our souls cry out, "What shall we do?"[16]

Do you hear Jesus' call and see your need of Christ? Indeed, the "right time" is now. Grieve over your sin and sinfulness and the devastation it has brought into your life. Confess the wrong you have done. This is the day of the Lord's favor. Today is the day of salvation.[17] This is your day to bow your knees, look up to your Father in heaven with a penitent cry, "Yes, Lord. Come Lord Jesus. I believe you are the Christ, my Lord and Savior." Receive the Scriptures you've just heard as the truth for your life and your eternity. Believe and be baptized in the name of the Father, and the Son, and the Holy Spirit. Then shout it out for all to hear!

Now, Jesus the Bridegroom is preparing you as a bride to enter into the joy of the Lord.

> *Behold, I stand at the door, and knock: if any man* [woman]
> *hear my voice, and open the door,*
> *I will come in to him, and will sup with him, and he with me."*
> (Revelation 3:20 KJV)

---

14. 1 Corinthians 15:3–5.
15. Matthew 11:28.
16. Acts 2:37.
17. 1 Corinthians 6:2.

24. Love is Knocking at Your Heart's Door
Q & A

1. Can you see the ruin of sin in your life and your need to come to Jesus Christ with a repentant heart?
   _____
   _____
   _____

2. Do you believe that Jesus is the Christ, Son of the Living God, Savior and Lord who has redeemed you from your sin debt?
   _____
   _____
   _____

3. Are you ready and willing to be baptized into Christ--His suffering, death, and resurrection?
   _____
   _____
   _____

4. Is there a longing in your heart to tell someone about the saving faith that has been given to you as a free gift?
   _____
   _____
   _____

My Jouural Notes:

The Greatest of These

As we wrap up this study, it's good to remember that many of the kingdom's precepts we are called to obey are impossible on our own. No matter how hard we try, fallen mortal beings simply can't love with the sincere love of Jesus.[1] Yet when we are made new creations in Christ and led by the Spirit, a heavenly bond of affection for our neighbor becomes totally possible.

We can't fulfill God's command to love by reinventing or reimagining it to fit our own likes and dislikes. It doesn't work to diminish love to suit our own taste and fit with our own desires. Heaven's love song writes lyrics on our hearts that are so much better than our own. We are a called and chosen people who delight in singing the greatest song in harmony with our Lord Jesus and heaven's angels.

Each of us expresses love in a way that is unique to us and our personalities. This is the joy of living just as the Good Lord made us. We express Christ's love that gathers us by separating us to Christ. This kind of affection connects us with a bond that has eternal staying power.

The Apostle Paul's life and ministry offers us an example of the greatest love in action. He was forgiven of his many sins as a persecutor of Christ and His Church. God's forgiveness compelled Paul to excel in love. This affection was constantly confirmed in his service as an apostle to the Gentiles. He worked tirelessly as God's bonded servant to preach the Gospel and establish churches on his missionary journeys. Because of his love for Christ, he endured many troubles, hardships, and distresses. He was beaten, imprisoned, and targeted by rioters. He spent sleepless nights wrestling in prayer for the churches. He went hungry, but still worked hard to minister in purity, understanding, patience, and kindness, sincere in the Holy Spirit.[2] This kind of sacrifice is its truest expression of godly affections, made possible because Christ first loved us.

The greatest love is immeasurable. Its vastness is more than the human mind can comprehend. This all-encompassing love brings godly order to home, work, community, state, and nation. It's as if the fragrance of love flows out from us to permeate everything and everyone we touch in Jesus' name.

God's tender nature is revealed in the Word of creation, evident in every day of Earth's creation. Our Creator entered His rest on the seventh day. With a great revelation of His Fatherly affections, He made a place for us in His rest—a place for all who will answer His call.

---

1. Romans 12:9.
2. 2 Corinthians 6:4–10.

Our Lord Jesus was born in a stable and placed in a cow's trough. He left the glory of heaven to show us how a humble servant shows love. His work ministering among us revealed a sacrificial, redemptive, and an all-encompassing bond of affection rarely ever known on earth. Jesus taught His disciples a love that serves and cares enough to discipline. In His life, suffering, death, burial, and resurrection, Jesus revealed to us the greatest love. Indeed, He was pierced for our transgressions.[3] This gift is given to us with a great promise of eternal life, wrapped in His everlasting love.

In the power of resurrection, we hold fast to love's promise. Because of Jesus' love, we are forgiven and saved from the curses of sin, Satan, and death. This awesome love, revealed to us in Christ, compels us to delight in obedience to His word. We will no longer drive nails into Jesus' hands by our willful sin. The depth of this mystery is higher, deeper, wider, and longer—beyond what human knowledge can comprehend. This eternal love fills us to the measure of the fullness of God.[4] Heaven's love gives us ears to hear, puts flesh on dry bones, and breathes the Spirit into those who have lost all hope.

God's love is the greatest love, and it is written on our hearts. Because of God's love for us, He disciplines those who break His covenant. This great, covenantal love makes it possible to love the unlovable simply by choosing to love them with the love of Christ.

Let us gather in Jesus' name to sing a new song of His love in harmony with the angels. May the wind of their wings touch and surround us as we join in singing heaven's love song.

> *And now these three remain: faith, hope and love.*
> *But the greatest of these is love.*
> *Follow the way of love and eagerly desire gifts of the Spirit.*
> (1 Corinthians 13:13, 14:1)

---

[3]. Isaiah 53:5.
[4]. Ephesians 3:18–19.

No eye has seen

No ear has heard
No mind has imagined
What God has prepared for those who love him.

But to us God revealed this by his Spirit.

For his Spirit searches out everything and reveals God's mysteries.

(1 Corinthians 2:9–10)[5]

---

5. Author's paraphrase.

Study Supplement
Learner-Guided Study

Every chapter of this study guide offers the learner an opportunity to gain in Biblical understanding and grow in grace and knowledge of our Lord Jesus Christ. Now, each student should have progressed enough to tackle an unguided study. This will be just you or your study group, the Word and the Teacher, who is the Spirit of Jesus.

First, read each verse. Pray and meditate on that verse. Consider the scripture in context. Look up associated passages in the Bible. Then, write what you learn. The following verses speak on the topic of the greatest love ever known. These Scriptures alone will change your mind and attitude of heart. Take them to heart and live in accord with them every step of every day. When you misstep, confess your failing, for our God is quick to forgive, to show mercy, to cleanse, and renew our fellowship with Him, for He is our Abba Father who is in heaven. Indeed, "The Lord is gracious and compassionate, slow to anger and rich in love."[1]

Your study challenge for this supplement is Romans 13:8–12. Write down your meditations, cross references, and study notes on each of the following Scriptures:

> *⁸ Let no debt remain outstanding, except the continuing debt to love one another, for whoever loves others has fulfilled the law.*

Notes:
_____
_____
_____

> *⁹ The commandments, "You shall not commit adultery," "You shall not murder," "You shall not steal," "You shall not covet," and whatever other command there may be, are summed up in this one command: "Love your neighbor as yourself."*

Notes:
_____
_____
_____

---

1. Psalm 145:8.

¹⁰ *Love does no harm to a neighbor. Therefore love is the fulfillment of the law.*

Notes:
_____
_____
_____

¹¹ *And do this, understanding the present time:*
The hour has already come for you to wake up from your slumber,
because our salvation is nearer now than when we first believed.

Notes:
_____
_____
_____

¹² *The night is nearly over; the day is almost here.*
So let us put aside the deeds of darkness and put on the armor of light.

Notes:
_____
_____
_____

Appendix
Definitions of Words as They are Used in This Study Guide, with Applicable Scripture References

Adonai

Translated as "Lord," This is a divine name, a sign of His sovereignty.

- "Therefore, you are to love *Adonai* your God and always obey his commission, regulations, rulings and *mitzvot*."[1] (Deuteronomy 11:1 CJB)

Advocate

Our Advocate is Jesus Christ who serves as our High Priest to intercede before the Father on our behalf. This is similar to a lawyer who pleads our case before a judge. Jesus promised to send another Advocate for our comfort—the Holy Spirit.

- "My dear children, I write this to you so that you will not sin. But if anybody does sin, we have an advocate with the Father--Jesus Christ, the Righteous One." (1 John 2:1)

- "Even now my witness is in heaven; my advocate is on high." (Job 16:19)

- "If you love me, keep my commands. And I will ask the Father, and he will give you another advocate to help you and be with you forever—the Spirit of truth." (John 14:16–17)

Aleph Tav

In Revelation 1:8, the Lord God says; "I am the Alpha and Omega." This is Greek for the Aleph (א) and Tav (ת). Aleph is the first letter of the Hebrew alphabet, and the Tav is the last letter. Aleph means beginning or commencing. This phrase includes connotations of the Almighty, the Breath, the Outermost, and the Center. Tav is a mark that separates us to the promised New Jerusalem.

- "Go throughout the city of Jerusalem and put a mark on the foreheads of those who grieve and lament over all the detestable things that are done in it." (Ezekiel 9:4)

---

1. Mitzvot: The Lord's command to be carried out as a sacred duty.

Assembly

A gathering of two or more followers of Christ who come together to worship, serve, and minister in the presence of the Lord in Jesus' name.

- "And let us consider how we may spur one another on toward love and good deeds, not giving up meeting together, as some are in the habit of doing, but encouraging one another—and all the more as you see the Day approaching." (Hebrews 10:24–25)

Atonement, Atoning Sacrifice

Those who were once separated are reconciled by the shed blood of Christ and brought into a loving covenantal union with the Father by means of Jesus' atoning sacrifice. The penalty for our sin's offense is paid in full because of Jesus' shed blood on the cross. We become blood-bought children of our Heavenly Father. We are adopted as children of the Most High God and given a new family name.

- "God presented Christ as a sacrifice of atonement, through the shedding of his blood—to be received by faith. He did this to demonstrate his righteousness." (Romans 3:25)

- "For this reason he had to be made like them, fully human in every way, in order that he might become a merciful and faithful high priest in service to God, and that he might make atonement for the sins of the people." (Hebrews 2:17)

Bride of Christ

The Church universal is the bride of Christ. All disciples of Jesus Christ throughout the world are one, and betrothed to the Bridegroom. At the wedding supper of the Lamb, all people who are parts in Christ's body are the Church and wedded to the Messiah.

- "I saw the Holy City, the new Jerusalem, coming down out of heaven from God, prepared as a bride beautifully dressed for her husband." (Revelation 21:2)

Bridegroom

Christ Jesus is the Bridegroom and the bride-in-waiting is the Church. We are compelled to keep alert and continue to watch for the Bridegroom's arrival with sufficient oil for our lamps as we wait, because we don't know the day or the hour of His return.[2]

---

2. Matthew 25:1–13.

- "Jesus answered, 'Can you make the friends of the bridegroom fast while he is with them? But the time will come when the bridegroom will be taken from them; in those days they will fast.'" (Luke 5:34–35)

Congregation

This is a gathering or assembly of two or more people in Jesus' name for the purpose of worship, serving, and ministering before the Lord. This gathering may include singing of Psalms, hymns, spiritual songs, and the ministries of teaching, preaching, prayers, and intercessions. This meeting often includes gathering around the Lord's Table to commune with Him, remembering His body broken and blood shed for the remission of our sins, to make us whole in body, soul, and spirit.

- "My feet stand on level ground; in the great congregation I will praise the LORD." (Psalm 26:12)
- "Praise God in the great congregation; praise the LORD in the assembly of Israel." (Psalm 68:26)

Covenant

Creator God is a God of covenants. The Hebrew noun בְּרִית, "bᵉrîyth," means to swear an oath, like the rainbow of seven colors that appeared after the flood.[3] Those who are in covenant with Christ break bread with Him at His table. The covenants God cuts with us are mutual, and yet we do not decide their terms. God created Adam and Eve and cut a covenant with them in the garden. The Great I AM gave a covenant of Law and Commandments for His nation, Israel, to safely guide them. In the age of the Church, we have a covenant that reveals Christ, provides redemption and an eternal promise. This is a covenant of love, grace, and mercy. Jesus calls us to keep covenant with Him, saying, "If you love me, you will keep my commandments."[4]

- "This is my blood of the covenant, which is poured out for many for the forgiveness of sins." (Matthew 26:28)
- "Because of this oath, Jesus has become the guarantor of a better covenant." (Hebrews 7:22)

---

3. Genesis 9:11.
4. John 14:15 ESV.

Creed

A confession of Christian faith, often proclaimed together in an assembly to affirm and declare the reason for the eternal hope we hold in our heart and soul. The words of a creed are sure principles and foundational precepts that reaffirm in our heart and mind the truths we embrace. The Apostle's Creed and the Nicene Creed are examples of creeds of the Christian faith.

- "Let us hold fast the confession of our hope without wavering, for he who promised is faithful." (Hebrews 10:23 ESV)
- "Through Jesus, therefore, let us continually offer to God a sacrifice of praise—the fruit of lips that openly profess his name." (Hebrews 13:15)

Disciple

Many disciples followed Jesus and twelve followed Him from the beginning of His ministry until the day of His resurrection. Eleven of those disciples became apostles to serve the early church. Today, all those who come into covenant with Jesus Christ as Lord and Savior and are called by His holy name are made disciples of Christ Jesus.

- "Then Jesus said to his disciples, 'Whoever wants to be my disciple must deny themselves and take up their cross and follow me.'" (Matthew 16:24)
- "And if anyone gives even a cup of cold water to one of these little ones who is my disciple, truly I tell you, that person will certainly not lose their reward." (Matthew 10:42)

Flesh, Sinful Nature, Human Nature

Adam came to life as the Spirit breathed into the man God had formed from the dust of the ground. Although they were perfectly created, Adam and Eve became corrupted by their sin in the garden. Because of this original sin, any person's nature can be dominated by sinful desires of the flesh or overruled by the power of the word and the Holy Spirit who dwells in His "temple." Our human nature gets weary doing what is right and good, but we must overrule the flesh by the power of the Spirit who is strength in us.

- "Watch and pray so that you will not fall into temptation. The spirit is willing, but the flesh is weak." (Matthew 26:41)
- "Therefore, brothers and sisters, we have an obligation—but it is not to the flesh, to live according to it. For if you live according to the flesh, you will die; but if by the Spirit you put to death the misdeeds of the body, you will live. For those who are led by the Spirit of God are the children of God." (Romans 8:12–14)

Gospel, Good News

The essence of the Gospel is Christ Jesus, the Word of Creation. He offered Himself as a sacrifice to be crucified, to die in our place, and pay the penalty for our sins. Jesus Christ, the Lamb of God, paid sin's penalty because all people have sinned, and sin's penalty is death.[5] The Gospel's redemptive message is possible because of Jesus' life, death, and resurrection. All those who are given ears to hear, hearts that repent, come to see the truth, and believe by faith have peace with God the Father.

The angels declared Good Tidings to shepherds who then hurried to Bethlehem to see the newborn Jesus. When Jesus began His ministry, it's as if every step He took brought Him closer to Jerusalem where He would offer up His body to be broken and His blood to be shed, so that we might be made whole in body, soul, and spirit. When Jesus ascended into heaven, He commissioned all His disciples to take this Good News to all the world, to teach and baptize in Jesus' name. God provided a way of redemption through His only Son, Christ Jesus who gave His life as a ransom for many. The Gospel will be preached to every tribe, nation, people, and culture before the end comes.[6]

This is the Gospel of peace,[7] the Gospel of grace,[8] the Gospel of our salvation,[9] and the Gospel of the glory of Christ.[10] The Gospel is revealed to us in three eyewitness accounts of Jesus teaching, and the signs and wonders performed during His life and ministry as Immanuel, God with us. The manifest presence of our Lord Jesus Christ is revealed in our midst when the true Gospel is preached, heard, believed, and obeyed. Indeed, the greatest miracle of all is wrought by the Gospel of Jesus Christ as a lost soul is forgiven, redeemed, and baptized into Christ, "so that in Him we might become the righteousness of God."[11]

- "I bring you good news that will cause great joy for all the people. Today in the town of David a Savior has been born to you; he is the Messiah, the Lord." (Luke 2:10–11)
- "For I am not ashamed of the gospel, because it is the power of God that brings salvation to everyone who believes: first to the Jew, then to the Gentile." (Romans 1:16)

---

5. Romans 3:23, Romans 6:23.
6. Revelation 7:9, Matthew 24:14.
7. Ephesians 6:15.
8. Acts 20:24.
9. Ephesians 1:13–14.
10. 2 Corinthians 4:4.
11. 2 Corinthians 5:21.

Jubilee

The sound of a trumpet called God's Covenant nation, Israel, to observe a Jubilee year that pointed the way forward to the Messiah. After seven sabbatical years came the Jubilee, or 50th year, when all slaves were set free, prisoners released, debts forgiven, and land returned to the family of the ancestral owners. It was also called the year of release. Jesus proclaimed this Jubilee to be satisfied in full as he read Isaiah's prophecy in the synagogue. Then He proclaimed; "Today this scripture is fulfilled in your hearing."[12]

- "The Spirit of the Lord is on me, because he has anointed me to proclaim good news to the poor. He has sent me to proclaim freedom for the prisoners and recovery of sight for the blind, to set the oppressed free, to proclaim the year of the Lord's favor." (Luke 4:18–19)

Judgment

God's just and righteous judgments are provided as a means of discipline to bring His people to repent. The Lord's judgments strengthen the bond of our covenant relationship with the Father, Son, and Holy Spirit. God's justice is according to all truth, revealing His nature as Supreme Judge—King of the nations.[13] Jesus will be the final judge of all humankind at the end of time, where every person must give account of what they have said and done.

- "When the Son of Man comes in his glory, and all the angels with him, he will sit on his glorious throne. All the nations will be gathered before him, and he will separate the people one from another as a shepherd separates the sheep from the goats. He will put the sheep on his right and the goats on his left." (Matthew 25:31–33)
- "His [Jesus'] winnowing fork is in his hand, and he will clear his threshing floor, gathering his wheat into the barn and burning up the chaff with unquenchable fire." (Matthew 3:12)

Kingdom of Heaven

The Kingdom of heaven is wherever God's will is done. Christ Jesus, the Prince of Peace, reigns over His people in righteousness, and under His rule we enjoy the blessings of His sovereignty. In the kingdom we find great rest and peace.

- "Again, the kingdom of heaven is like a merchant seeking fine pearls, and upon finding one pearl of great value, he went and sold all that he had and bought it." (Matthew 13:45–46)

---

12. Luke 4:21
13. Revelation 15:3.

- "To him who loves us and has freed us from our sins by his blood, and has made us to be a kingdom and priests to serve his God and Father—to him be glory and power for ever and ever! Amen." (Revelation 1:5–6)

Living Sacrifice

All Christians are called to live their lives as a sacrifice before the Lord. This means that we think of others more highly than ourselves.[14] We consider the needs of others as great or greater than our own. The desire of God's heart takes precedence over our personal desires. The desires of the flesh are surrendered so that we may fulfill God's purpose and plan for our lives. We give our strength and energies to do the work God has ordained for us. We are made holy in Christ and we present ourselves as a holy sacrifice before the Lord.

- "Therefore, I urge you, brothers and sisters, in view of God's mercy, to offer your bodies as a living sacrifice, holy and pleasing to God—this is your true and proper worship." (Romans 12:1)
- "For we are God's handiwork, created in Christ Jesus to do good works, which God prepared in advance for us to do." (Ephesians 2:10)

Long-Suffering

Our sin not only causes us to suffer, it causes our Lord God to suffer.[15] But the Lord is patient with us. He is faithful to His promises even when we are not faithful to keep covenant with Him.[16] The Lord God is merciful, willing to wait for the day of our awakening so we may repent of our sin against Him.

- "In all their distress he too was distressed, and the angel of his presence saved them. In his love and mercy he redeemed them; he lifted them up and carried them all the days of old." (Isaiah 63:9)
- "But you, Lord, are a compassionate and gracious God, slow to anger, abounding in love and faithfulness." (Psalm 86:15)

Lord's Table

The bread and cup are the feast set before us on the Lord's Table. These are the elements of communion and we are partakers of Christ as we partake of Jesus. The bread is Jesus' body, broken that we might be made whole in body, soul, and spirit. The cup is Jesus' blood, shed for the forgiveness and cleansing of our sins. As we come to the Lord's Table, we reaffirm the covenant that makes us one with Him, and one with all who are called by Jesus' holy name.

---

14. Philippians 2:3.
15. Jeremiah 8:21.
16. 2 Timothy 2:13.

- "For I received from the Lord what I also passed on to you: The Lord Jesus, on the night he was betrayed, took bread, and when he had given thanks, he broke it and said, 'This is my body, which is for you; do this in remembrance of me.' In the same way, after supper he took the cup, saying, 'This cup is the new covenant in my blood; do this, whenever you drink it, in remembrance of me.' For whenever you eat this bread and drink this cup, you proclaim the Lord's death until he comes."
(1 Corinthians 11:23–26)

Love

The Greek word for love is ἀγαπάω, "agapáō." This is the heart and soul of Christian faith, and the greatest of all godly attributes. God's law of love is written on our hearts, and it's a higher standard than the commandments chiseled in stone. The Greek word has connotations of self-sacrifice, provision, chosen, harmony, serving, and bonding.

- "Whoever does not love does not know God, because God is love. This is how God showed his love among us: He sent his one and only Son into the world that we might live through him. This is love: not that we loved God, but that he loved us and sent his Son as an atoning sacrifice for our sins. Dear friends, since God so loved us, we also ought to love one another." (1 John 4:8–11)

Loving Kindness

This precious word in Hebrew is חֶסֶד, "cheçed," and it reveals the Creator's nature. This is the essence of all the covenants the Great I AM makes with His people. This word offers connotations of, loyalty, duty, care, truth, and trustworthiness, all emanating from God's loving nature. God's loving kindness goes hand in hand with His mercy.

- "I am unworthy of all the kindness and faithfulness you have shown your servant. I had only my staff when I crossed this Jordan, but now I have become two camps." (Genesis 32:10)
- "One thing God has spoken, two things I have heard: 'Power belongs to you, God, and with you, Lord, is unfailing love.'" (Psalm 62:11–12)

Mercy

Mercy: ἔλεος, "éleos," forbearance from inflicting punishment on an adversary or a covenant breaker. Mercy is compelled by God's compassion for the weak, the sick, and the spiritually impoverished. Mercy is shown in acts of kindness for those who suffer. In mercy, God provided a "Lamb" as a sacrificial offering to die in our place, for our sin, and for our salvation.

- "But because of his great love for us, God, who is rich in mercy, made us alive with Christ even when we were dead in transgressions—it is by grace you have been saved." (Ephesians 2:4–5)
- "Have mercy on me, LORD, for I am faint; heal me, LORD, for my bones are in agony." (Psalm 6:2)

Mount Zion

Mount Zion and the new Mount Zion are two of seven hills that surround Jerusalem. The writer of Hebrews leads us to worship on Mount Zion in the city of the living God. This is the place we ascend to exalt the Lord and sing with the angels in joyful assembly. Heaven's mountain is the altar where Jesus Christ, our High Priest, mediates our covenant before God who sits on the throne.[17]

- "But you have come to Mount Zion, to the city of the living God, the heavenly Jerusalem. You have come to thousands upon thousands of angels in joyful assembly." (Hebrews 12:22)

Redemption, Redeemed

Those who are impoverished, weak, broken, victimized, imprisoned, and sick are set free from the clutches of darkness. Jesus Christ is Redeemer who declares freedom for the captives and opens the eyes of the spiritually blind. Jesus paid our ransom so that we might be redeemed, no longer captives to sin. Christ the Redeemer is foreshadowed in Old Testament times by kinsman redeemers who had the right to redeem the property of a near relative.[18] All those who come to saving faith are called the redeemed of the Lord.[19]

- "The Spirit of the Lord is on me, because he has anointed me to proclaim good news to the poor. He has sent me to proclaim freedom for the prisoners and recovery of sight for the blind, to set the oppressed free, to proclaim the year of the Lord's favor." (Luke 4:18–19)
- "For even the Son of Man did not come to be served, but to serve, and to give his life as a ransom for many." (Mark 10:45)

Repentance

Repentance is an essential step on the way to saving faith, a change of heart and mind toward God. A contrite heart breaks when convicted of sin, then we confess our wrong and turn from our disobedience. By the power of the Word and the work of the Holy Spirit, our hearts and minds come into agreement with truth and turn away from the sin that destroys us.

---

17. Jeremiah 3:17.
18. Ruth 2:20, 4:14
19. Isaiah 62:12.

- "Peter replied, 'Repent and be baptized, every one of you, in the name of Jesus Christ for the forgiveness of your sins. And you will receive the gift of the Holy Spirit.'" (Acts 2:38)
- "He told them, 'This is what is written: The Messiah will suffer and rise from the dead on the third day, and repentance for the forgiveness of sins will be preached in his name to all nations, beginning at Jerusalem. You are witnesses of these things.'" (Luke 24:46–48)

Sacrament

This word doesn't appear in the Bible. The word Sacrament comes from the Latin *sacramentum*, which means an oath of obedience to an authority. This is used to describe holy rites of worship in the church, such as Baptism and the Lord's Supper. These are regarded as the principle rites of worship in the church today; also referred to as ordinances of the church.

- "We were therefore buried with him through baptism into death in order that, just as Christ was raised from the dead through the glory of the Father, we too may live a new life." (Romans 6:4)
- "While they were eating, Jesus took bread, and when he had given thanks, he broke it and gave it to his disciples, saying, 'Take and eat; this is my body.' Then he took a cup, and when he had given thanks, he gave it to them, saying, 'Drink from it, all of you. This is my blood of the covenant, which is poured out for many for the forgiveness of sins.'" (Matthew 26:26–28)

Salvation

This is what God does on behalf of sinful, fallible human creatures who can put forth no effort of their own except to open the door when Jesus knocks.[20] The Lord's redemptive work is illustrated in historic Biblical accounts of Yehovah's holy nation, Israel. God's saving grace is the promise of salvation—our eternal hope. The revelation of God's plan of salvation began with Adam and Eve in the garden, and continues into the Apostle John's Revelation, where the hope of our salvation comes to fruition. The promise of our salvation is ever-present with us in Christ, and the fulfillment of our salvation manifested as Christ is fully revealed at the end of time. God saves us, calling us out of darkness into the light of life.[21] In Christ, we are brought into fellowship with God by His only Son, Jesus Christ.[22] By saving faith, we become sons and daughters of the Most High God, and we are given a new family name.

---

20. Revelation 3:20.
21. 1 Peter 2:9.
22. 1 Corinthians 1:9.

- "And having chosen them, he called them to come to him. And having called them, he gave them right standing with himself. And having given them right standing, he gave them his glory." (Romans 8:30 NLT)
- "Repent, then, and turn to God, so that your sins may be wiped out, that times of refreshing may come from the Lord, and that he may send the Messiah, who has been appointed for you—even Jesus." (Acts 3:19–20)

Sanctuary

A holy place, a tabernacle or temple for God's holy name where His people gather to worship. God provides this place of safety where His people may find rest. The tabernacle Moses built in the wilderness served as a type or illustration of the true sanctuary in heaven. Heaven's sanctuary is where Christ Jesus serves as High Priest and offers Himself as a sacrificial offering.

- "We do have such a high priest, who sat down at the right hand of the throne of the Majesty in heaven, and who serves in the sanctuary, the true tabernacle set up by the Lord, not by a mere human being." (Hebrews 8:1–2)

Saving Faith

This is to trust in the Lord Jesus Christ as Lord and Savior, having faith to believe and be baptized in the name of the Father, Son, and Holy Spirit. Saving faith is a gift given to us through holy words. Life-giving words of the Scriptures are the means by which we come into the light of Christ and eternal life in glory. Noah's life provides us a beautiful illustration of this saving faith. It is by faith that we come to trust and rely on God's promised salvation.

- "By faith Noah, when warned about things not yet seen, in holy fear built an ark to save his family. By his faith he condemned the world and became heir of the righteousness that is in keeping with faith." (Hebrews 11:7)

Saving Grace

This is one of the most beautiful phrases in the Bible. It offers connotations of joy, delight, favor, charm, sweetness, kindness, mercy, and redemption; all given to undeserving souls. Grace is the kindness of God toward unworthy people.

- "But because of his great love for us, God, who is rich in mercy, made us alive with Christ even when we were dead in transgressions—it is by grace you have been saved." (Ephesians 2:4–5)

Sin, Sinner

Sin is any act or inaction that is contrary to holiness and a violation of our love covenant with the Father. All sin is against the Lord and an affront to a holy God. The penalty of sin is death, and sin's death sentence was paid by our Lord Jesus who gave His life to die in our place. In His vicarious death, burial, and resurrection, He overcame sin, Satan, and death. Anything we do that does not come from faith is sin.[23] We are all born into sin because of Adam's original sin. We are all sinners in need of forgiveness, cleansing, and saving grace.

- "Against you, you only, have I sinned and done what is evil in your sight; so you are right in your verdict and justified when you judge." (Psalm 51:4)
- "There is no difference between Jew and Gentile, for all have sinned and fall short of the glory of God, and all are justified freely by his grace through the redemption that came by Christ Jesus." (Romans 3:22–24)

Soulish

Soulish people often call themselves Christians but allow their natural mind, human reasoning, inborn instincts, personal emotions, and willfulness of the soul to rule over their body and spirit. They have not conformed their minds to Christ,[24] and they are not circumcised of heart.[25] They are people who will not submit to the authority of the Spirit of Christ. Indeed, their lives, words, and deeds come from the natural mind, human emotion, and willfulness of the flesh. They cannot receive from the Spirit of God because their soulish nature rules over them. This kind of person will not have a teachable spirit.

- "The natural person does not accept the things of the Spirit of God, for they are folly to him, and he is not able to understand them because they are spiritually discerned." (1 Corinthians 2:14 ESV)

Holy Spirit, Spirit of Christ, Spirit of Jesus, Spirit of God

The Hebrew word for the Holy Spirit is רוּחַ, "rûwach." The wind of the Spirit moved over the surface earth's dark and formless waters on the first day of creation. Then, on the sixth day, the Spirit breathed into Adam's body made from the dust of the ground and he became a living soul. Again, in Noah's day, the Spirit breathed upon the flood waters to make them recede and to renew the earth for Noah's family and all the animals on the ark.

---

23. Romans 14:23.
24. 1 Corinthians 2:9–10, 16.
25. Romans 2:25–29.

The spirit of man is evident when, on the day Jesus ascended to heaven, He breathed on His disciples to give them life in His righteousness. The Word of creation, the Breath of the Almighty, breathed on the disciples, who became new creations in Christ. Then the Holy Spirit came as a mighty rush of wind to establish the church in all who were gathered to pray on the day of Pentecost.

- "Jesus said, 'Peace be with you! As the Father has sent me, I am sending you.' And with that he breathed on them and said, 'Receive the Holy Spirit.'" (John 20:21–22)

- "You, however, are not in the realm of the flesh but are in the realm of the Spirit, if indeed the Spirit of God lives in you. And if anyone does not have the Spirit of Christ, they do not belong to Christ. But if Christ is in you, then even though your body is subject to death because of sin, the Spirit gives life because of righteousness. And if the Spirit of him who raised Jesus from the dead is living in you, he who raised Christ from the dead will also give life to your mortal bodies because of his Spirit who lives in you." (Romans 8:9–11)

Temple of the Holy Spirit

All blood-bought sons and daughters of the Most High God are a sacred dwelling place—a temple where the Holy Spirit resides. The Spirit of Christ doesn't dwell in a place polluted by willful idolatry. Instead, God's Spirit dwells in the temples of all those who are forgiven, cleansed, washed, restored, and redeemed. We offer our bodies as a living sacrifice where the Spirit of Jesus may dwell, all for the glory of God.

- "God's temple is sacred, and you together are that temple." (1 Corinthians 3:17)

- "Flee from sexual immorality. Every other sin a man can commit is outside his body, but he who sins sexually sins against his own body. Do you not know that your body is a temple of the Holy Spirit who is in you, whom you have received from God? You are not your own; you were bought at a price. Therefore glorify God with your body." (1 Corinthians 6:18–20)

Yeshua HaMashiach

This is the historic Hebrew title conferred on Jesus by the Father. The Greek translation is Christos. This name means "Christ the Anointed One and Jesus the Messiah." Yeshua is the prophet of whom Moses prophesied when he came down from the mountain after he received God's commandments. Joshua, who led the tribes of Israel across the Jordan River into the Promised Land, was a type of Christ and was also called by the name Yeshua.

- "The Lord your God will raise up for you a prophet like me from among you, from your fellow Israelites. You must listen to him." (Deuteronomy 18:15)

Yehovah, Jehovah

This is a name of God found in the historic Hebrew language. Written Hebrew showed no vowels, so this name is penned as JHVH. Some Hebrew academics believe Yahweh is the proper way to say this name. Traditional Jews do not say the name aloud because they consider it too holy for any person to speak.

- "And I appeared unto Abraham, unto Isaac, and unto Jacob, by the name of God Almighty, but by my name Jehovah was I not known to them." (Exodus 6:3 KJV)

www.ingramcontent.com/pod-product-compliance
Lightning Source LLC
Chambersburg PA
CBHW072004110526
44592CB00012B/1196